Comparative Studies in Software Acquisition

Lexington Books Series in Computer Science

Kenneth J. Thurber, General Editor

Basic Computer Logic
John R. Scott

Comparative Studies in Software Acquisition
Steven Glaseman

Computing in the Humanities
Peter C. Patton and Renee A. Holoien

Data Base Computers
Olin H. Bray and Harvey A. Freeman

Database Management System Anatomy
James A. Larson

Data Structures and Computer Architecture
Kenneth J. Thurber and Peter C. Patton

Distributed Database Management Systems
Olin H. Bray

Distributed-Processor Communications Architecture
Kenneth J. Thurber and G.M. Masson

Interconnection Networks for Large-Scale Parallel Processing
Howard J. Siegel

Local Networks
W.R. Franta and Imrich Chlamtac

Microcomputer Interfacing
G. Jack Lipovski

Requirements-Oriented Computer System Design
Kenneth J. Thurber

Software Blueprint and Examples
Yaohan Chu

User-Designed Computing
Louis Schlueter, Jr.

Comparative Studies in Software Acquisition

Management Organization versus the Development Process

Steven Glaseman
Teledyne Systems Company

LexingtonBooks
D.C. Heath and Company
Lexington, Massachusetts
Toronto

Library of Congress Cataloging in Publication Data

Glaseman, S.
    Comparative studies in software acquisition

    Bibliography: p.
    Includes index.
    1. Computer programming management.   I. Title.
QA76.6.G557   658.4'0388   81–48559
ISBN 0–669–05422–4   AACR2

Copyright © 1982 by D.C. Heath and Company

Published simultaneously in Canada

Printed in the United States of America

International Standard Book Number: 0–669–05422–4

Library of Congress Catalog Card Number: 81–48559

To Mary Jaynne

Contents

List of Figures
and Tables

Figures

Tables

Preface and Acknowledgments

This book extends the results of a Rand Corporation study, sponsored by the U.S. Air Force, of software requirements for computers embedded in weapons systems.

As a study of the software acquisition management aspect of eight major system acquisition projects, this book touches areas of interest to a variety of groups, including the defense, industrial, and research communities, and spanning both the public and private sectors of the economy. Within that extended population, this material should be particularly relevant to those who now, or will in the future, manage large software-involved acquisition programs, to those who provide policy guidance for such tasks, to systems and software engineers who must accomplish the work, and to a subset of educators: those who teach the systems engineers and analysts and those who teach their management counterparts.

Acknowledgments

Although there is one name on the cover, many individuals contributed in various ways to the work represented by this book. In the next few paragraphs I will try to thank as many of you as I can remember. To those I have forgotten to mention, please forgive my temporary lapse.

I am indebted to Dr. Arthur Alexander, associate head of the Economics Department at Rand, for his contribution to the intellectual focus of this work. His friendly enthusiasm and cogent advice provided much-needed support at several crucial points along the way.

I also owe considerable thanks to Professor Rein Turn of the California State University at Northridge and Dr. Willis Ware of Rand for their thoughtful guidance and encouragement. Willis was also my department head at Rand during the time I spent writing this book. I am grateful for his administrative support during that period and for the benefit of his experience with the Air Force's software milieu. Dr. Steve Lukasic, chief scientist at the Federal Communications Commission, was an early discussant, and I thank him for several direction-setting conversations.

Throughout the production of this book Ms. Suzi Jackson smiled a lot, thereby lessening my guilt as I submitted draft after marked-up draft to her outstanding word-processing skills. My debt to Suzi's expertise and friendship is enormous. I also thank Ms. Dee Saenz for keeping things going at those times when there was too much work for Suzi to handle alone. For the financial support of parts of Suzi's and Dee's work I am grateful to Dr. Charles Wolf, Jr., dean of the Rand Graduate Institute, and, until recently, head of Rand's Economics Department.

I also owe thanks to Mr. Steve Drezner, vice-president for Rand's Project AIR FORCE, for assigning me the project that eventually grew into this book. Mr. Mal Davis, Mr. Bob Reinstedt, and Dr. Bill Faught, all Rand colleagues, each helped with that project and each encouraged my efforts to extend its results. The value of their support is hard to overestimate.

Ms. Barbara Quint and Ms. Shirley Lee have given me a new appreciation of the importance of reference librarians. Their unfailing good cheer and professionalism were a great help to me, and I thank them for that.

Dr. Robert Anderson was my department head for much of my Rand Graduate Institute experience. His encouragement, sympathetic ear, and lobbying efforts on my behalf are gratefully acknowledged.

More Air Force officers, enlisted personnel, and civilians than can be listed here contributed their skills, experiences, and insights to these pages. They know who they are, however, and they have my profound thanks. Two individuals must be mentioned. Colonels Robert Ziernicki, since retired, and John Marciniak are due special thanks for their tireless efforts to illuminate the Air Force's information-technology problems and to initiate and support a number of research programs, including those leading to this study.

Thanks are also due my colleagues at Teledyne Systems Company. Mr. Harry Halamandaris, president, and Mr. James Fithian, vice-president for engineering, both supported the stretch run to get the manuscript to the publisher on time.

Finally, I must thank my family. To my parents, Mr. and Mrs. J.B. Glaseman of San Mateo, California, I owe the obsessive personality required for a project of this sort. I am grateful also for their encouragement and support. I have four children; all of them—Shane, Mindi, Keith, and Chelsi—have put up with a part-time father (with, at times, a serious attitude problem) for several years. I will probably never be able to repay my debt to their cheerful acceptance of my obsession. They have my deepest thanks, and will soon have more of my attention.

My wife, Mary Jaynne, has been through nearly twenty years of marriage to a student. The youngest person in spirit that I know, she has an apparently bottomless reservoir of cheer, good will, and, above all, tolerance. Mary Jaynne made it all possible, and any attempt to express the debt I owe her would be grossly inadequate.

1 Introduction

This book is concerned with the fact that, for computer systems of any size or complexity, the management of software development is frequently an Achilles heel. The view taken in these pages is that some of the important management problems are rooted in organizational structures and procedures that are inappropriate to actual software development practice.

Software emerged as an issue during the 1960s. At that time, concern was based on mounting evidence that the techniques employed to program computers for ever-more-complex tasks produced expensive, and often inadequate, products. In the commercial world, examples were advanced operating systems and computer-aided design systems. At the same time, the military—particularly the Air Force—had begun to employ digital computers in its newest weapon systems. By 1968, the collection of approaches for dealing with software had been given a name—software engineering—and had begun to attract individuals interested in advancing the field in a systematic way (Naur and Randell 1968).

Since the 1960s, much work has been done. Predictably, we have tried to segment, diagram, analyze, and automate everything in sight. To date the results are mixed, but there have been some obvious advances in both theory and in practical application. Perhaps the best publicized examples are in the areas of structured techniques for software analysis, design, and coding (McGowan and Kelley 1975; Yourdon and Constantine 1975; DeMarco 1979) and in the use of chief programmer teams (Baker 1972). However, a much broader set of topics is also under scrutiny, including, for example, automated aids to requirements analysis (Bell et al. 1977), language standardization (Fisher 1976), hardware "family" standards (Burr et al. 1977), software engineering education (Wasserman and Freeman 1978), program verification (Good, London, and Bledsoe 1975), and program testing (Howden 1978).

The management aspects of this new discipline are also being studied. Much of the literature in this area addresses corporate- and line-management shortcomings encountered on large software projects; these include the following (Ware 1978):

Loose or nonexistent management oversight and control.

Uneven application of standards.

1

Lack of relevant management experience.

Lack of an overall engineering approach.

Although the majority of management-oriented research is addressed to problems in the industrial sector, large software projects are undertaken in several very different environments. For example, software development for large, commercially acquired management support systems (for example, computer operating systems, corporate data management systems, process control systems, and so on) is usually managed by a hierarchy of corporate staff communicating upward from ''software project leader'' to, say, ''vice-president for systems development.'' A quite different environment is created when the latter structure is in turn overlaid by the convoluted plexus of Defense Department agencies and offices that is associated with acquiring a military computer system. This augmentation by external agencies of a contractor's internal management structure reflects certain rarely articulated differences between defense software and its commercial relatives. It often leads to a situation wherein Defense Department actors ''manage the managers'' (Douglas 1980). In this book, we will examine the effect of this management approach on the outcomes of defense software development projects and, in so doing, come to some conclusions about software acquisition management in general.

There are some risks in deriving broad conclusions from a study whose examples are all drawn from defense system acquisitions—primarily Air Force weapon systems of the 1970s. However, the research was focused by the environment in which it was carried out and not by the uniqueness of defense—as compared to non-defense—software problems. For the organizational and managerial issues which are the primary concerns of this book, the similarities may very well outweigh the differences.

Consider that weapon system software projects differ from other software development projects in the following characteristics:

Software requirements for weapon system computers are defined not only by information processing concerns but also—to a greater extent than for other kinds of software—by the overarching requirements of the larger Defense products in which they are embedded.

Weapon systems take longer, on the average, to reach deployment than do other systems; an eight- to eleven-year development cycle is not unusual. Such lengthy projects tend to incur ''on-the-fly'' modifications in response to changes that occur in critical parameters during that period as a result of technical progress, new requirements, different threats, and so on.

Weapon system software, as a class, is dominated by requirements for real-time, virtually error-free (or, at least, fault-tolerant) operations. This kind of software is arguably the most challenging form of the art.

The management environment surrounding weapon system software acquisition is often more complex than in other areas. The resulting push and pull of competing incentives, traditions, political sensitivities, and experiences generates a milieu in which crisp and timely decisions are sometimes hard to obtain.

It is important to understand that these characteristics are not of equal importance, that they do not operate at the same levels, and that they contribute effects both individually and in combination according to the circumstances of individual acquisition programs. In the aggregate, therefore, while they have an effect on the day-to-day management of any defense software project, the specific effects are largely idiosyncratic. Evidence can be found in the uneven history of successes and failures in defense software acquisitions of the past two decades.

More important than what distinguishes weapons systems from other software projects are the elements they hold in common. The following similarities seem to apply across the board, not only to weapon system software, but to a majority of large software development projects.

Software development proceeds along quite similar lines, whatever the nature of the product. For example, most contractors use (or are testing) structured techniques for analysis, design, and coding; management and client walkthroughs and reviews at various stages of the development cycle; and formal integration and testing programs at all levels of product completion.

Troublesome software products exhibit common symptoms, regardless of the kind of system being developed. The most frequently encountered symptoms have changed little in the last twenty years: excessive cost growth, slips in delivery schedules, and less than satisfactory initial performance. (See, for example, Hosier 1961, DeRoze 1975, and Douglas 1980.)

Common symptoms are seen as having common antecedents. Frequently encountered are faulty or incomplete treatment of requirements; poor software literacy on the part of management; few tools to aid software development; and failure to transfer lessons learned from one project to the next. (See also House 1980 and Glass 1980.)

A wide variety of successful software products share common developmental traits. These traits (among others discussed in greater detail later on) are early software prototyping (Peters 1978); earlier attention to software than is usual during system definition; and nonstandard treatment of documentation.

These similarities have less to do with the technological details of individual software projects than with the overall industry approach to software development and to its management. ("Industry" here includes those DOD actors who become deeply involved with development management—for instance, a system program office.) These similarities in the broader issues of process and management permit cautious generalization to software environments outside the bounds of the cases studied here.

Embedded Computers

An *embedded* computer is defined as in integral component of a larger system whose major functions go beyond data processing. Such computers are often physically embedded in the systems they support, as in aircraft, missile weapon systems, and modern microwave ovens. Physical proximity is not, however, necessary to the definition. Many systems employ computers that, embedded in the functional sense, nonetheless are physically separated from other operational components (for instance, air-traffic-control systems).

In a sense, of course, most computer installations are embedded in larger systems. Payroll and accounting systems, for example, are sub-components of the larger corporate structure they help to support. Similarly, computers that support research-and-development environments, automated industrial design facilities, point-of-sale and inventory-control systems, and many other different activities are embedded in larger systems whose overall purposes—according to the above definition—go beyond data processing.

Over the past decade, embedded computers have assumed an increasingly important role in national defense. Designed into modern weapon systems, computers perform, monitor, and integrate many critical functions. For example, table 1–1 lists the major functions that on-board computers perform in a contemporary fighter aircraft. Resulting improvements to system capabilities, performance, and operational simplicity

Table 1–1
Major Functional Categories for On-Board Computers

Executive control of the computational subsystem
Navigation
Guidance
Stores management
Electronic warfare subsystem control
Targeting/fixtaking
Controls/displays processing
Communications
In-flight system test

carry the price tag of increased complexity in the computational subsystem. Just as in non-defense systems, the software component is a major source of such complexity.

When first introduced, software was treated as an unimportant developmental detail, to be provided whenever necessary by the appropriate contractor. Those involved in system acquisition believed that software required little explicit attention in terms of acquisition management techniques, so there was no pressure to examine those techniques. Today, however, we know that software's concepts, design, and development characteristics must be seen as important decision variables in their own right.

This is true for several reasons. First, each new system is more dependent on software than its predecessors. Figure 1–1 illustrates this point—again, for military aircraft. It shows that the amount of on-board storage capacity has increased one-hundred-fold over the last twenty years—a doubling of capacity every three years or so. Although some of this capacity is used for data storage, the overwhelming majority is required for on-line storage of increasingly large and complex computer programs—software.

Second, over these same twenty years there has been a tremendous growth in software costs. Table 1–2 traces the percentage of total computing system costs represented by computer hardware and software for all Defense Department computer systems. These costs reflect all aspects of software: design, development, testing, operation, and life-cycle support. The ratio of hardware to software costs has changed from four to one in the mid-1950s to almost one to four in early 1980. Current estimates are that the ratio will approach one to nine within four years.

The actual amount expended on defense software currently runs at approximately $7 billion per year, with an estimated increase to $12 billion within four years. As shown in table 1–3, Air Force systems by themselves account for nearly half of the yearly DoD software investment.

Finally, as is suggested by the previous points, software as a tech-

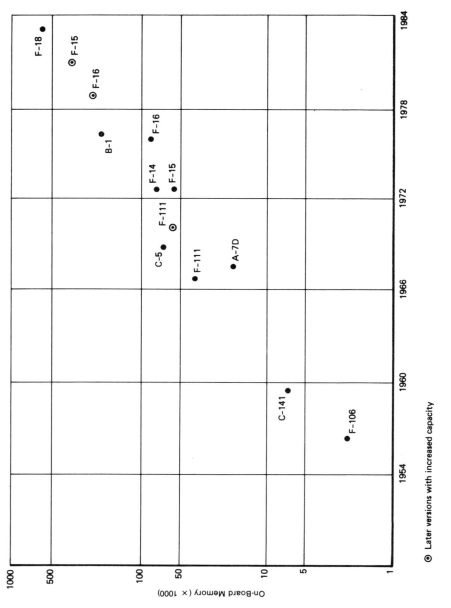

On-Board Memory (× 1000)

⊙ Later versions with increased capacity

Figure 1–1. On-Board Storage Capacity (Military Aircraft)

Table 1–2
Cost Trends: Hardware versus Software
(percentage of total costs)

	1955	1970	1979	1985 (Estimate)
Computer Hardware	83	45	25	10
Software	17	55	75	90

Source: Various estimates in recent literature.

Table 1–3
Software Investment: DOD and USAF
(billions of dollars)

	1979	1985
Total DOD Software	7	12
Embedded DOD Software	5.25	10+
USAF Embedded Software	3	5

Source: Various estimates in recent literature.

nology—its techniques, tools, procedures, and capabilities—is progressing at an extremely rapid pace. It requires a correspondingly responsive organizational environment to keep up with this progress, let alone derive maximum benefits from it at any point in time.

Moreover, as software technology advances, more and more opportunities are created for its use. This pressure has resulted, for many modern systems, in a situation where software determines performance. This is particularly true of defense systems—if the software fails, all or part of the mission it supports also fails. The Air Force's new F-16 fighter is a good example. Most of this aircraft's mission functions—target detection, navigation, weapons release, and so on—are supported by specialized computers interfaced with one another to form a complete, functionally integrated weapon system. Soon, even its flight surfaces will be digitally controlled. Pressures from the pilot's stick will be digitized and transmitted to a computer that, after certain comparisons and adjustments, will pass the results to control surface actuators. It is easy to see that software problems translate directly into reduced mission capability. Other examples can be drawn from modern commercial aircraft, from military command and control systems (see the NORAD example, below), and from a variety of communications systems.

In the remainder of this book, software development management will be discussed in the context of the Defense Department's software acquisition life-cycle. This focus is dictated by the study on which the book is based, and gives the advantage in clarity to readers familiar with that context. As I have argued above, however, the results of the study are applicable, in various degrees, to a broader audience. They extend, with minimal translation, to the software acquisition environments of other agencies of the federal government and, with somewhat more but still moderate effort, to state and local government projects, and to the private sector.

Defense System Acquisition

The government acquires major systems primarily by contracting with a special subset of the commercial sector. The relationship can be described as a partnership between a prime contractor and the government in which the former has the major responsibility for system design and development and the latter monitors progress and tries to assure tracking with overall system requirements. The partners share responsibility for testing and for identifying and resolving problems.

Defense contractors are often asked to develop systems that may require significant technological advances. As a result, the contractor community has built up a wealth of specialized organizations, tools, expertise, and experience to bring to bear on their responsibilities. This is particularly true in the software area. Table 1–4 depicts the growth in the personnel devoted to software-related tasks at one contractor over the last twenty years.

The Problem

As the software they are asked to develop has grown more complex, contractors' capabilities have also grown. Of course, this growth has not been smooth. Some programs have been canceled, others redirected, and many—because of their priority—pursued in the face of significant cost growth, schedule slippages, and performance shortfalls in the delivered system. (A few important development programs have had value as learning exercises.)

Table 1–4
Trends in Contractor Resource Assignment
(percentage of development personnel)

	1960 (F–4)	1970 (F–15)	1980 (F–18)
Noncomputer hardware	98	74	57
Embedded computer hardware	1	2	3
Embedded software	1	24	40

Source: Personal communication, McDonnell Douglas Aircraft Company.

Overall, the record of recent software acquisition experience favors the contractors. They continue to produce and sell systems, to grow, and to demonstrate most of the signs of successful market performance. The government, however, is frequently dissatisfied with the results of their eight-to-eleven year partnership with industry. It may also face an extended period of inflated life-cycle support costs, because the software will need continuous modification and updating to guarantee a system's operational utility for a "reasonable" period of time.

The program to update the North American Air Defense (NORAD) command and control facility provides a concrete example of these problems (U.S. Government Accounting Office 1978). The objective was to improve mission performance by replacing the computer hardware and software and, at the same time, to enhance systems supportability by using more recent, and thus more available, technology. The program was initiated in 1969 with funding approved at $90.6 million. It was to become operational in 1976. As of early 1979, its cost overrun had exceeded 100 percent, its schedule had slipped by three years, and it had failed to meet a number of the originally approved performance specifications. The system satisfies a reduced set of specifications, but these define capabilities not functionally superior to the early 1960s technology it is replacing. Thus, after 11 years and at a cost of over $200 million, the Air Force has replaced 20-year-old technology with 10-year-old technology, achieving little or no operational benefit and only a marginal improvement in supportability. For the NORAD program, many of these troubles are laid squarely on the doorstep of software development.

Whatever the proximate causes—and these vary from system to system—the problems of software cost growth, slipped schedules, and less-than-anticipated performance characterize a large number of defense acquisition programs. In particular—with one or two important exceptions—most of the major systems the Air Force acquired during the 1970s had such problems to some extent. The software problem, therefore, is widespread, and it has been with us essentially undiminished for the better part of two decades.

A number of studies have been directed to various aspects of this problem (Johns Hopkins University Applied Physics Laboratory 1975; MITRE Corporation 1975). Most focus on certain technical aspects of software development, including the following:

Structured techniques for design and development (Yourdon and Constantine 1975).

Requirements analysis aids (Bell et al. 1977; Teichroew et al. 1975).

Language standardization (Fisher 1976).

Hardware "family" standards (Burr et al. 1977).

Yet, despite many studies, and despite some important contributions in specific areas of software engineering, the government's software acquisition problems persist—seemingly unaffected by the resources applied to their resolution. This suggests that we have yet to deal with the fundamental issues. Many of what are now described as problems may, instead, be symptoms.

Roots of the Problem

Three points from the earlier discussion, taken together, provide some clues about where to look for more fundamental problems. First, the user's most frequent complaint is not that software doesn't perform; rather, it is that its performance does not match the needs that exist when the system is delivered. Since it is the government's responsibility to communicate its requirements and to insure that changes in requirements are adequately reflected in the development contract, inadequate acquisition management by the government may be partially to blame for user dissatisfaction.

Second, the government's current approach to software acquisition management evolved during a time when hardware was the primary concern. The use of digital computers in weapon systems came about as a gradual infusion of, and commitment to, digital technology. System software was treated as a low-level developmental detail to be provided, wherever necessary, by the contractor. Defense program managers were not suddenly presented with a new and unfamiliar set of problems; standard management tools seemed to apply as well as before. But the rate of employment of embedded computers increased rapidly after this initial period. By 1974, it was generally agreed that severe performance, cost, and schedule problems had resulted from the government's failure to perceive that their growing dependence on software was accompanied by complex new management requirements.

Finally, the very rapid pace at which information technology advances adds to the government's management problem. To keep up with such rapid evolution requires, as was noted earlier, a correspondingly responsive organizational environment.

These observations suggest the following hypothesis:

Many of the problems in acquiring embedded software are rooted in organizational structures and procedures that are inappropriate to actual software development practices.

In other words, many of the symptoms mentioned earlier may be caused by problems in organizational adaptation. If this is true, it suggests that the problem might be attacked by searching out policy actions that, once adopted, would produce more successful project outcomes as natural consequences of fundamentally improved management practices.

The Research Approach

The approach to evaluating this hypothesis is based on an examination of eight major acquisition programs drawn primarily from the Air Force Aeronautical Systems Division and Electronics Systems Division. Each program involves a substantial embedded computer component. Interviews were conducted with personnel from each system program office (see Putnam [1972] for a useful description of this management concept) and with personnel from each contractor organization, with emphasis on the individuals in each group who deal with software acquisition. From this data base, chronologies were developed for both the software acquisition management process and the software development process associated with each program. These chronologies are the primary basis for the analyses and conclusions presented in subsequent chapters. The information was augmented and validated as much as possible by additional interviews and discussions at the Air Force Wright Avionics Laboratory, at the Second, Third, and Fourth U.S. Air Force Armament and Avionics Planning Conferences, and with colleagues in the research community. System and program management information was made available on the condition that only aggregate results would be reported. In particular, we agreed not to discuss the details of any single program or to encourage direct or implicit association of specific programs with any issues under discussion. Thus, results are presented here without the system-specific information upon which they are based and the chronologies in appendixes A and B have been modified to remove information that would reveal the identities of the systems discussed.

It is important to note that system acquisition studies of this type focus on a moving target. The programs under study began at different times (although their development life-cycles overlap to varying degrees); they represent different stages of maturity in the relevant technologies; and they have, at this writing, reached different stages in their evolution. The fact that it is nevertheless possible to form a relatively stable picture of Air Force software acquisition management practices suggests their sluggish response to an environment in which operational concepts and technologies advance at a very rapid rate.

Existing studies in software acquisition management tend to deal with specific issues such as cost estimation techniques (Marks 1980; Air Force Avionics Laboratory 1977; Glore 1978), technical visibility (Driscoll 1976; Barbee 1978), and program structure (Losi 1977). Considering such studies in the aggregate, we find that most of the fundamental principles underlying the acquisition management process are under scrutiny. This reflects a well-documented and long-standing dissatisfaction with current practice; it also suggests, by a conspicuous lack of results, that it may be the "glue" that is at fault and not the individual components of management.

In this case, the glue corresponds to the organizational framework that ties the personnel, tools, and techniques of management together into an integrated whole. Accordingly, we have guided our analysis of the case-study data by certain propositions extracted from the recent literature on organizational adaptation (see chapter 2). We then use them to compare software developent as reflected in Air Force management activities with software development as actually practiced by defense contractors.

This study deals with three different models of the software development process. The first model, described in chapter 3, pertains to the software development process as it is actually carried out by defense contractors. We examined the contractors who were developing software for the eight systems under study.

Chapter 4 describes two additional models. That chapter's primary objective is to describe the software-development process implicit in Air Force acquisition-management practices. Accordingly, the first part of chapter 4 gives a general overview of program office management practices in order to place the reader in context. This is followed by a more focused analysis of the case-study chronologies mentioned earlier. Only software-related program office behavior is examined, and common practices are identified as key management activities. Activities are then compared across all programs and certain characteristics are highlighted to indicate how those involved appear to structure the software development process.

These characteristics are collected, organized into categories, and used to construct a model of the software development process that the Air Force is managing.

Chapter 4 also draws attention to (but does not dwell upon) another model of software development—that embodied in official Air Force guidance, most notably Air Force Regulation 800–14. This third model is relevant to questions of how, and how well, policy guidelines influence organizational behavior. Chapter 4 touches briefly on the match between the software development process as embodied in official Air Force regulations and the model, mentioned earlier, implied by Air Force behavior.

Our attention, however, is focused on comparing the first two models. Chapter 5 draws out a number of discrepancies between actual software development and the process being managed by the Air Force.

In chapter 6, impediments to widespread change in Air Force management practices are explained in terms of existing organizational policies, traditions, and politics. We then discuss programs that made such changes and the incentives that led them to do so. This chapter also examines recent evidence for improved results in one recent program that is being managed under an implicit model more in accordance with the actual software development process.

Chapter 7 makes a number of recommendations for changes in existing policies that, if implemented, could provide an improved organizational basis for managing future software acquisitions. Of course, implementation is a key question here and, although a thorough analysis is beyond the scope of this book, some observations are given based on the author's experience. Finally, we briefly discuss other applications of the results presented here.

2 Organizational Adaptation

Hawley (1950) recognized thirty years ago that organizations engage in activities whose sole objectives are adjustment to environmental pressures. This idea was formalized with the rise of general systems theory and with the observation, most persuasively made by Katz and Kahn (1966), that organizations could be viewed as open systems. That is, organizations, rather than being closed, self-sufficient entities, are systems open to influence from the outside. They have certain dependencies on their environment and, therefore, must manage those dependencies and adjust to changes in their environments in order to survive. (This is an oversimplified description of an important concept; the interested reader is referred to Katz and Kahn [1966] for more detail.)

Over the last fifteen years, mainstream research on organizational adaptation has given much attention to definitional issues. Many writers have developed typologies of organizations (Hughes 1952; Parsons 1960; Blau and Scott 1962; Katz and Kahn 1966; Etzioni 1975), and some have considered which organizational forms seem most adaptable (in some sense) to environmental change. Ansoff and Brandenberg (1971), for example, identify four basic organizational forms that have endured over the years and that are therefore presumed to have adapted well to their environments. They characterized these four forms in some detail, their intent being to furnish a sort of checklist for organizational designers to use in selecting a form appropriate to a given environment. However, the procedure for using their approach is largely intuitive. The connections between specific environmental demands and a given set of organizational objectives are unique enough to require modifications to the basic forms. The choice and implementation of these modifications are left to the designer.

A number of studies have also been devoted to defining the aspects of environments that have special relevance for adaptive organizations. Sethi (1970) suggests that environments are composed of a number of structures—physical, social, ecological, legal, and so on—all of which bear in some way on the survival of organizations embedded in them. Emery and Trist (1965) have developed a typology of environments that has generated considerable interest. According to this work, there are four "ideal" types of environments, one of which, the turbulent field, seems closely related to the complex and dynamic interdependencies that characterize some modern organizations. In a similar vein, Thompson's concept of the heterogeneous-dynamic task environment is part of a very creative effort to describe environmental characteristics that influence the structure and processes of organizations (Thompson 1967).

Few of these works, however, lay down rules for *how* environmental elements—however defined—influence organizations, nor do they pinpoint the aspects of organizations that are most sensitive to such influences. Thus, although there is general agreement that organizations must and do adapt to changing environmental conditions, and although various definitions, typologies, and taxonomies have been created for both organizations and environments, relatively little has been learned about how such adaptations take place. Research emphasizing organizational characteristics has not shown which characteristics are most sensitive to external influences, nor how such influences affect specific characteristics. From the other direction, most environmentally oriented work stops short of identifying specific environmental components as particularly influential, and has yet to develop the important mechanisms of such influence.

Part of the reason for this situation is that there is, as yet, little agreement as to which of the many alternative descriptive variables—for either organizations or environments—are most useful. However, certain variables do appear in most discussions and thus represent at least some degree of consensus. One of these is organizational structure. However it is defined, and by whatever mechanism it changes, structure is always one of the variables that is seen to change—to adapt—as the environment changes.

In an early paper, however, Starbuck (1965) notes that structure changes only gradually and cannot be expected to respond to rapid short-run environmental fluctuations. Similarly, Blau and Scott (1962) observe that organizations can often be quite slow in modifying their structure to be more consistent with environmental demands. Chandler's thesis that "structure follows strategy" is based on a view that organizational strategy and, thus, structure is set in part by considering environmental demands (Chandler 1962). He is also quick to point out that unresponsive organizational structures lead to what he calls a management by crisis approach. In this mode, managers defer decision making in certain areas until some event makes a decision necessary (by then usually remedial). These and similar writings suggest broad agreement with the following general observations:

1. Structural change is one important way in which organizations adapt to changes in their environment.

2. Organizations may have trouble making rapid structural changes in response to rapid environmental changes.
3. Where adaptation is slow, inefficiencies may develop that lead to discretionary management practices.

Technology is another central idea in the adaption literature. Originally, it referred to the application of machines to tasks earlier performed manually—that is, to technology as automation. Social scientists, however, also became interested in the effects of technology on the social aspects of organizations (Trist and Bamforth 1951; Miller and Rice 1963). Over the years, the concept of organizational technology has grown in scope, in complexity, and in influence. Joan Woodward's seminal work in this area related technology to a broad set of organizational variables (Woodward 1958, 1965, 1970). Changes and extensions were developed in the Aston studies (Hickson et al. 1969; Pugh et al. 1969) and the Child studies (Child and Mansfield 1972; Child 1973). Organizational technology embraces a large number of task-related activities and resources available to an organization and is essentially synonymous with the concept of process.

The importance of this idea, along with its roots in organizational structure, suggests that technology plays an important role in adaptation. Thompson's (1967) propositions relating the constructs of organizational domain (Levine and White 1961) and task environment (Dill 1958) to organizational behavior can be interpreted from this perspective. The environment, for Thompson, represents uncertainty, and organizations—since they strive to be rational actors—must reduce uncertainty in order to be effective. Thus, different organizational technologies, or processes, are employed in uncertainty-reducing ways to help an organization adapt to environmental influences. Thompson also related his notion of technology to an organization's structure. Certain structures are suited to certain types of uncertainty-reducing processes. This theoretical integration of organizational structure, process, and environment suggests its potential importance to our concerns here.

We will therefore guide our analysis of how well the Air Force's acquisition-management organization has adapted to rapid changes in software technology by the following two propositions:

The larger and more complex an organization, the slower its structure adapts to environmental change.

The larger and more complex an organization, the slower its processes adapt to environmental change.

There is, on the other hand, ample evidence that not all large and complex organizations have trouble adapting to rapid environmental shifts; most germane to the present study are the defense contractors. We have previously noted their ability to keep fairly well in tune with the rapidly advancing technologies associated with modern defense systems (computers and communications technologies are two important examples). However, these organizations seem relatively stable in structure and process; what seems to adapt is the attentional mechanism, a concept only recently emphasized in the organizational literature.

Interestingly enough, the notion that organizations "pay attention"— that is, focus on some, but not all, of the information available to them— also stems from research in uncertainty reduction. Weick (1969) suggests that organizations create their own environments as a function of the perceptions of their members. In this view, the environment to which an organization adapts is only a part of the whole, which suggests that adaptation to unperceived aspects of the larger environment is unlikely. Pfeffer and Salancik (1978) are motivated by this work to suggest that an external observer can enhance his understanding of organizational behavior if he takes this attentional process into consideration.

This way of thinking about environmental response focuses attention on the concept of information. Only those aspects of an organization's environment to which it pays attention can contribute information useful for the organization's activities. An obvious danger is that, as an organization evolves, certain originally insignificant and unperceived aspects of its environment will gradually grow in importance until they are crucial to survival, and that the organization, paying no attention to them and collecting no relevant information, will be unaware of problems until the major impacts are felt.

Pfeffer and Salancik also note that attentional processes are set by existing organizational structure and processes at any point in time. Weick, on the other hand, considered his notions about the created environment as more relevant to initial organizing behavior than to the behavior of in-place organizations. In either case, there seems to be general agreement that attentional and informational mechanisms are useful concepts, along with structure and processes, for improving our understanding of how organizations adapt to their environments. The following proposition, therefore, will be included in the analytic framework:

Attentional and informational mechanisms are central to an organization's ability to adapt to change.

The three propositions introduced in this chapter lead to specific questions that guide the analysis in chapter 5. Before posing those questions, however, it is necessary to introduce, in the next two chapters, the observations that provide substance for that analysis.

3

The Industry's Software Development Process

It is important in what follows to distinguish among the various actors involved in the system acquisition process. A large number of organizations play important roles at various times; figure 3–1 indicates the most important of these and something of their interrelationships. The shaded boxes represent the two organizations with which we are concerned: the Air Force System Program Office (SPO) and the prime industrial contractor. These two are the chief actors concerned with the acquisition of software embedded in Air Force systems.

Basically, the prime contractor has responsibility for system design and implementation, including components and subsystems that may actually be supplied by subcontractors. In the software area, for example, the prime contractor has overall responsibility to the Air Force for the entire software package, for overseeing and coordinating his own and subcontractor programming efforts, and for integrating the results with the products of other development efforts (for instance, hardware) to produce the desired system. The prime contractor's approach to software development is further discussed below.

The SPO typically does not develop software, nor does it directly manage programming activities. Its task is one of linkage. Air Force mission needs typically change during the acquisition period, along with them change system requirements. Since contracts are based on requirements specifications, one of the SPO's major tasks is to ensure that approved changes are communicated to the contractor and coordinated with his ongoing activities. Thus, the SPO has a management perspective that is unavailable to the contractor but that is crucial to the cost-effective development and timely delivery of a useful product. The next chapter describes the top-level decision-making activities common to most of the eight program offices examined, from the earliest conception of the system up to the software Critical Design Reviews (CDRs) that precede the computer programming activity.

The question to be answered in this chapter is: What is the process actually employed by defense contractors when software development is required? To answer this question, we interviewed the prime contractors' software engineering managers for all eight of the systems in the sample. The results of each interview are presented in the form of software development chronologies in appendix B. The restriction to prime contrac-

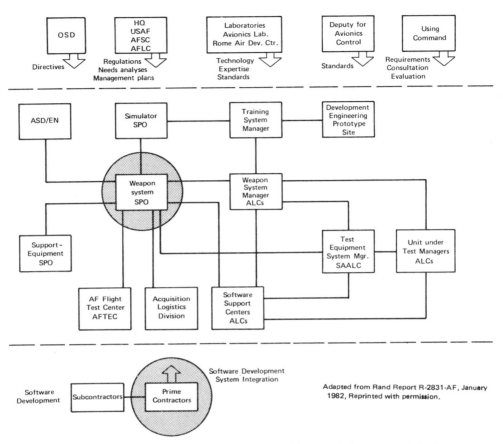

Figure 3–1. Major Organizations: Acquisition and Support of Software in Air Force Systems

tors was a result of the limited resources available to the study, but actually imposed no serious informational problems. For all but two of the systems involved, the prime contractor produced a major portion of the mission software; in all eight systems, the prime contractor was responsible for software integration.

Each chronology was analyzed for the fundamental set of activities making up a given contractor's approach to software development. This information was then used to develop a conceptual model of each contractor's process up to and including the critical design review. These models also appear in appendix B. The reader should keep in mind that the process examined below, although described in terms most relevant to the defense industry, applies as well to a spectrum of non-defense environments.

Figure 3–2 is a composite model based on the similarities among all the individual contractor models. The following paragraphs describe what can be considered a canonical model of software development. It is based primarily on Figure 3–2, but appeals to the chronologies in appendix B for implementation details not shown in the figure.

The Software Development Process

All of the contractors interviewed maintain a permanent group that pursues technological advances applicable to the contractor's interests. These groups are staffed by senior technical and marketing personnel; an increasing number of whom are formally trained in computer science. Essentially, these are research-and-development groups, operating primarily in a laboratory environment and more concerned with technical feasibility than with practicality. Their roles include providing technical information and demonstrations to support managerial postures that emerge during the contractor's dialog with the potential customer.

When, through this dialog, it becomes clear that the customer is moving toward an acquisition decision, appropriate members of the advanced technology group meet with corporate management personnel to consider the broad outlines of the anticipated program. This can occur several months to several years before a request for proposal (RFP) is actually released. These early discussions focus on developing technical information to support a decision on corporate participation in the program. Initially, attention centers on defining system-level characteristics such as size, weight, power, and complexity and on developing estimates of the corporate resources required and costs involved in pursuing a contract. Should the contractor decide to participate, discussions are continued in more specialized teams formed from the original group to focus attention on major subsystems. For example, an aircraft contractor might develop teams to examine airframe, propulsion, and avionics subsystems. For command and control systems, teams might form for communications, data processing, and display subsystems. Each team further defines its subsystem by considering past experience and new technologies, developing and experimenting with models, and making initial contacts with potential subcontractors. In this way, alternative designs for the computational subsystem are developed and evaluated, known constraints

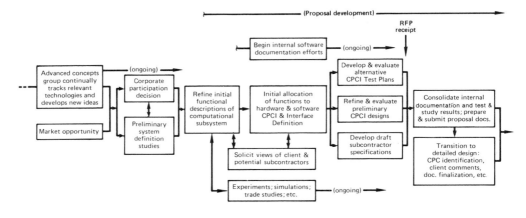

are assessed for their impacts on cost and performance, and mission information is gathered, all for use in allocating subsystem functions to hardware and software. Together, all these activities constitute the initial requirements definition and analysis steps as this concept applies to the computer resources envisioned for the system in question.

Attention to software is limited, at first, to allocative issues. Gradually, as past experience and new information are factored in, possible designs for each major software component are developed, reviewed, and coordinated among teams. Consideration then slowly shifts to issues of programming language, program size, interface characteristics, and module function. These issues arise naturally as system requirements become more and more specific. Thus, the evolution of software requirements implies and involves the postulation of software architectures or designs. These designs are then examined and evaluated; they are the conceptual tools of the software requirements analysis process. Each major software component is eventually associated with a list of functional requirements. This starts as an incomplete draft and evolves to a highly detailed formal specification as requirements respond to the continuous studies and analyses that characterize this period in the development process.

The contractor's teams come together often to summarize and coordinate their individual activities. By this process, problem areas are identified and new issues raised, some of which are returned to the teams

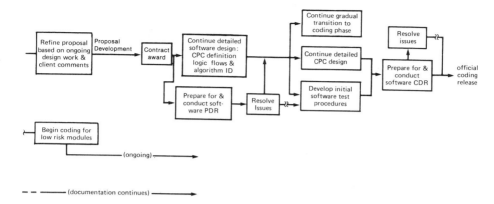

Figure 3–2. Composite Model: Contractor Software Development

for resolution. This cycle of team activity/joint review continues, in most cases, for one or more years. It runs parallel to and shares some information with the customer's efforts to come to an acquisition decision based on mission needs and budget priorities. In some cases, coordination may be formalized by demonstrations of technology or by development contracts for prototypes.

Thus, when a request for proposal (RFP) is finally released, the contractor community is usually well prepared to respond in detail. In the software area, for example, informal team documentation is collected, reviewed for consistency, and placed in a format very much like draft software development specifications. Such specifications typically identify a programming language, suggest the use of structured design and implementation techniques, and present a philosophy of programming dealing with modularity, data use, minimal complexity, and the like. They can also include early lists of functional requirements at the major subsystem level, interface requirements for functions within a given subsystem, subsystem interface diagrams, and even top-level flowcharts for some functions. Depending on the individual case, early drafts of a computer program development plan, interface control documents, and preliminary software product specifications might also be available.

The initial RFP can be for a system definition contract or for full-scale development. If a system definition contract is to precede the development phase, a different path is followed (discussed in a later chapter). If, as is normally the case, a development RFP is received, the contractor typically forms a proposal-preparation team. The technical part of the proposal is written by small groups, each addressing a specific functional area—for example, the target-acquisition task for a command and control radar. These groups are made up of participants in the contractor's system definition efforts, just described.

Each group produces what is often called an area specification. These are reviewed individually for technical accuracy and consistency and collectively for their responsiveness to the full set of requirements contained in the RFP. The resulting volumes are packaged with documents reflecting the financial management aspects of the contractor's proposal and then submitted to the potential customer.

While the customer (in our context, the Air Force) evaluates the proposal, the contractor's specialized groups continue their efforts in technical assessment, modeling and experimentation, subcontractor interaction, and documentation. In this way, subsystem design alternatives are refined, evaluated, and formalized as Configuration Items (CIs). This work, in conjunction with Air Force questions and comments, may lead to several modifications and refinements to the original proposal.

Once the contract is awarded, software design efforts move gradually from the computer program configuration item (CPCI) level to the computer program component (CPC) level. In a command and control radar, for example, once the general outlines of the target-acquisition subsystem are agreed upon, detailed attention can be given to software for the detection, recognition, and identification components that define it. Thus, the contractor begins a transition to the detailed design stage of software development. Simultaneously, preparations begin for a software preliminary design review (PDR). This usually involves internal reviews of functional and module-interface designs, preliminary test plans, and current strategies for software development. Available documentation is usually finalized, and is in any case submitted to the Air Force prior to the formal review. Preliminary development specifications, draft interface specifications, draft product specifications, and a computer program development plan may also be included. Senior technical and administrative managers may also conduct design walk-throughs. For software, this implies reviewing plans for eventual functional integration of individual subsystems. The contractor may also rehearse, preparing and conducting dry runs of the various briefings to be presented to the customer's review team.

Conceivably, a contractor may fail to satisfy the review team. In that case, he must resolve the problems leading to the failure and, when the problems are serious enough, schedule another preliminary review. Usually the issues raised are less serious, having more to do with management planning than with technical challenges. These issues are resolved and informally rereviewed by the customer as part of the technical interchange meetings normally scheduled between the time of the preliminary design review and the subsequent critical design review (CDR).

In theory, detailed software design follows approval (at the preliminary review) of the overall software design represented by the development specifications. Approval implies baselining or freezing the design; it is granted when the customer is satisfied that the overall functions, performance, interfaces, and structure envisioned for the software are compatible with and traceable to approved system-level requirements. Subsequent changes must be formally submitted and evaluated; if permitted, they are documented as part of the software-configuration management record begun upon approval of the design.

In practice, as already indicated, detailed software design may begin much earlier. At times, it may even begin before the development contract is awarded—when, for example, the contractor's specialized teams elaborate individual functional areas for the proposal package. This makes

Table 3–1
Software Development Characteristics Based on Actual Development Programs

Ordered Activities
System definition studies lead to overall system requirements and to functional breakdowns for each anticipated subsystem.
Computer subsystem definition flows from system definition studies. Experimentation, simulation, vendor contacts, and other studies are used to develop and evaluate alternatives.
Preliminary software designs emerge gradually as a function of the evolution and analysis of subsystem requirements, acceptable designs, and coordination with other system and subsystem components.
Software design elaboration receives increasing attention as largely informal analyses and design decisions are reevaluated, documented, given formal status, and compiled into a technical proposal.
Detailed software designs begin to appear as work continues to extend and elaborate upon selected preliminary software designs.
Programming and checkout begins in many cases prior to official reviews, based on the contractor's perception of schedule variables and technical risks and on the level of design achieved in each case.

Relationship to System-Acquisition Events
The software life-cycle begins at the same time as the system acquisition life-cycle.
Software acquisition activities span the system-acquisition process.
Software development runs parallel to, and is largely integrated with, the development of certain other system components.
Although several stages are discernable, a high degree of interdependence, iteration, and change are the essential characteristics of software development projects.

sense because the contractor, understanding that software is a major cost driver, needs to learn as much as possible about it in order to develop and submit cost estimates.

The emerging design details of each separate program module are documented in the software product specification, the contents of which are of primary concern at the critical design review. Therefore, as the module designs are refined and documented, the contractor begins to prepare for that review. These preparations are generally similar to those already described for the preliminary review; however, a critical review usually involves considerably more technical detail.

Problems discovered during that review are resolved by the design teams in charge of software components affected, with Air Force oversight through informal meetings. If no significant problems are found with the detailed software design, with its traceability to the approved development specifications, or with the available software product specifications, the contractor may proceed with coding. Again, practical considerations frequently dictate that coding begin prior to the critical review.

Table 3–1 summarizes the main characteristics of software development as undertaken by defense contractors. In a subsequent chapter, we will compare this process as actually carried forward with the model of software development projected by Air Force management practices. The next chapter develops the Air Force model.

4

Air Force Embedded Software Acquisition Management

It is difficult to identify the starting point of the system acquisition process. Programs emerge gradually from a background of continuous mission area analyses, planning studies, and research-and-development efforts undertaken by military and industrial organizations alike. Sometimes the surfacing of a new technological capability motivates interest in its mission-enhancing potential. At other times, a known and worsening operational shortfall eventually generates enough concern to support informal but focused examination of alternative solutions.

As the Air Force goes through the process leading to an acquisition decision, research-and-development activities within the contractor community intensify and focus on areas related to perceived Air Force interests. These separate and parallel activities are coordinated by frequent interaction between the two communities. Although these crucial early discussions often address technical issues, software (apparently because it is not viewed as a major component of system-level decisionmaking) is rarely a subject of detailed concern at this point in Air Force deliberations.

Formal initiation of system acquisition proceedings usually comes from an operational organization in the form of a document describing and justifying their needs. The next step is a review of this document conducted by Headquarters, U.S. Air Force. Many nontechnical factors affect review outcomes and influence subsequent program conduct—international trade agreements, treaties, political pressures, media pressures, lobbies, economic factors, defense posture, and national policy are some examples. It is also necessary that the review reconcile any proposed acquisition with other DoD capabilities, resources, and priorities. A positive review eventually results in a program management directive specifying how Air Force Systems Command should proceed with the acquisition program.

The Air Force is required to study and evaluate alternative concepts for satisfying the need and to submit the findings to DoD for approval. Studies that may be carried out include management, production, and support feasibility studies; concept of operation studies; cost/schedule and cost/effectiveness studies; and preliminary design studies for the major subsystems. Most studies are done by contractors, but occasionally study teams are formed within the Air Force.

These studies almost invariably focus on issues related to the system's primary mission. For aircraft, these issues are at the level of: How high? How fast? How destructive? They deal only infrequently with "collateral details" such as functions to be performed by software (National Academy of Sciences 1977). In any event, current Air Force guidance does not require the development and review of software cost and feasibility information. Moreover, even though the Air Force has both formal and informal relations with contractors, it shows little tendency to tap their software resources during these early system-level studies. As we saw, contractors (unlike the Air Force) pay considerable ongoing attention to the cost, size, feasibility, and so on of software, particularly during their early decision making with regard to proposal submission.

At this stage, recommendations by the newly formed system program office (SPO) are submitted for Defense Department approval before the Air Force actually commits itself to a full-fledged acquisition program. After approval, the first major task is to prepare a management plan and to develop an initial system specification. How well such tasks are done depends on a number of things, including: (1) the kinds of resources available to the SPO; (2) the experience of the contractor community; and (3) schedule and budget pressures. The initial studies mentioned earlier provide some insights for use as the program office prepares for the DoDs decision on proceeding to the development phase. In most of the programs we investigated, there was no evidence of substantive concern for software issues at this point.

Instead, attention is focused on preparing a request for proposal (RFP) for the development phase, as shown in figure 4–1. Current policy suggests, but does not require, that a large number of software-relevant issues be considered in developing the portions of the specifications that address system computational resources. For the programs examined, the software portions of the RFPs were contained in relatively few pages and dealt with, for example, the use of higher-order programming languages, the use of top-down structured design and programming concepts, early attention to interface requirements, and other quite general aspects of software development.

In this same timeframe, the SPO is required to produce a draft computer resources integrated support plan (CRISP). The requirements for soliciting and evaluating responses to a development RFP and preparing the CRISP seem eventually to motivate increased attention to software. Proposal evaluation is often supported by analyses of some of the technical

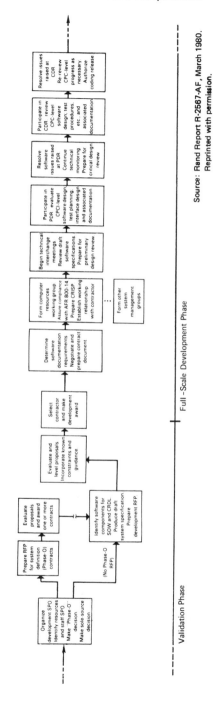

Figure 4–1. Aggregate Model (Partial): Embedded Software Acquisition Management

Source: Rand Report R-2567-AF, March 1980. Reprinted with permission.

and economic trade-offs among competing proposals. It is noteworthy that, for most of the programs examined, a contractor's past experience or demonstrated capability in computer or software technology was not a significant factor in the selection process.

After the development is awarded, the SPO enters a phase aimed at monitoring the contractor's managerial and technical progress and participating in various aspects of problem identification and resolution, test planning, and so forth. To perform this job well often requires the formation of specialized groups, each responsible for certain aspects of the development process. The computer resources working group (CRWG) is one such group, although its members are concerned primarily with the computer resources support plan mentioned above. Few of the programs examined had formed any other group that dealt primarily with software development management or with other aspects of the computational subsystem.

Seven of the eight programs went directly from contract award to the software preliminary design review (PDR) in a period of at most three months. This review is intended as an opportunity for the Air Force, first, to detect any misunderstanding in the contractor's translation of the relevant system-level requirements into a preliminary software design and, second, to evaluate his ability to actually produce a satisfactory software product. Issues addressed range from inadequate documentation to—in rare cases—design rejection. In any event, the Air Force assigns action items to monitors on the program office staff. Resolution is defined either as problem solution or as an acceptable plan for future solution. Depending on the magnitude of the problem, resolution can be accepted informally by letter or can precipitate a repeated review. Once all software issues raised by the review are resolved, the software development specifications are approved and the contractor is expected to proceed with the detailed design.

Before actual program development begins, the SPO must evaluate the detailed software design at a critical design review (CDR) and approve (or take issue with) the contractor's work up to that point. The value of this review, as with the earlier one, depends on the software expertise of the SPO staff. To the extent that more technically complex information is under review, more sophisticated staff is needed to mount a technically adequate critical design review.

As before, problems discovered during this review are resolved by the contractor, and the results are monitored through technical-exchange meetings. In theory, if no significant problems are found, the contractor then begins to code the computer programs themselves.

Implications for a Model of Software Development

The purpose of this section is to describe the SPO's involvement in software acquisition in order to infer its perception of the software-development process. Most writers in this field agree that the system acquisition life-cycle consists of five stages, starting with the conceptual stage and ending with the operational stage (see figure 4–2). All major subsystems of a given system are considered to traverse these five stages, including the software developed for embedded computer resources. This section addresses the following questions about software-acquisition management, neither of which have been adequately considered in earlier studies:

1. What process is the Air Force managing?
2. How does that process relate to the model of software development upon which current policy is based?

Software Acquisition-Management Activities

The activities described here (see table 4–1) are those undertaken by virtually all of the program offices in the sample. Together, these activities represent the Air Force's attempt to exercise some measure of control over the contractor's software-development process. Presumably, each activity is related to one or more specific components of the software development process as perceived by the Air Force. In other words, these activities, considered together, imply a model of software development. The purpose of this section is to derive that model.

After we examine how a given activity was carried out by personnel in each program office, we will direct our attention to characteristic behaviors that indicate how Air Force managers view the software-de-

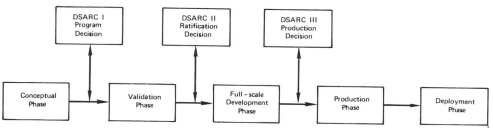

Note: DSARC = Defense System Acquisition Review Committee.

Figure 4–2. Phases of System Acquisition Process

Table 4–1
Key Activities: Software-Acquisition Management

Assign system program office (SPO) computer resources staff
Prepare software content of request for proposal (RFP) package
Form computer resources working group (CRWG)
Participate in system design review (SDR)
Participate in software preliminary design review (PDR)
Establish baseline software development specification (SDS)
Initiate software configuration management
Participate in software critical design review (CDR)

velopment process. These behaviors focus on step-wise attention to specific events (see table 4–1) that are perceived as milestones in the contractor's software development process.

Activity 1: Assignment of System Program Office Computer Resources Management Staff. This activity occurs during the formation of the SPO, when a positive decision on system acquisition is anticipated. The first objectives of this initially small (two- to three-person) group are to provide the computer-related content for a development RFP (see Activity 2) and to form the nucleus of a computer resources working group. Air Force regulations (U.S. Air Force 1971, 1975) suggest that available software technicians and managers be identified and their roles discussed in management planning documents, and that both formal reviews and technical-interchange meetings be staffed by personnel with computer expertise. It should be noted that, although the regulations were not in full force when programs A through D were being initiated, their outlines were visible in early 1973. The thinking they represented was therefore available to the managers of programs initiated after 1973 or still in the early decisionmaking stages at that time (this encompasses systems D through H of the systems studied here).

For six (A through F) of the eight programs studied, the assignment of the computer resources staff constituted the first explicit recognition of the software content of the program. Thus, one might reasonably conclude that this event, together with the subsequent attention to software matters, represented the beginning of the software life-cycle from the point of view of the Air Force.

Software acquisition emerged as a major issue within the Air Force at approximately the time that three influential studies about software became available (Johns Hopkins University Applied Physics Laboratory 1975; MITRE Corporation 1975; Drezner et al. 1976). All three identified poor information and experience transfer as important problems in the software-acquistion area. Yet, in those programs that might have been expected to respond to these studies the SPO staff made no attempt to identify or gain access to potentially useful information from past or concurrently active programs, inside or outside the Air Force. This suggests software managers for major new acquisitions consider their tasks unique enough to diminish the value of recent experience relative to the costs of access to such information. In effect, program office software managers act as though they hold the following two views:

The software life-cycle begins when the system life-cycle enters the phase of full-scale development.

Each new software development effort is unique enough to diminish the value of available experiential data.

Activity 2: Preparation of the Software Content of the System Specification, the Statement of Work (SOW), and the Contract Data-Requirements List (CDRL). This activity is usually undertaken as soon as the necessary staff is acquired; its objective is to supply computer resources content for the evolving development RFP. The work is usually done by a group made up of SPO software staff, supported by available personnel from the participating commands and from the relevant defense contractor community.

There are, as yet, few published and approved data item descriptors (DIDs) for computer software, although work is underway to implement and test a recent MITRE Corporation recommendation in this area (Byrne et al. 1978). There is not yet general agreement as to what information about the software-development process should be required as deliverable by contract. In five of the eight programs studied, the software content of the development RFP (including the statement of work, the contract data requirements list, and the system specification) was very sparse. In two of those cases, less than ten pages out of several linear feet of procurement package documentation dealt explicitly with software.

This suggests that it has been acceptable to the program office to field an RFP that lacks substance in an area vital to the success of both the development effort and the ultimate defense mission. In four programs (A through D), the Air Force contracted for software-relevant studies as input to their efforts to write a system specification. In two other programs, studies were begun prior to the development decision and were fed into the RFP once the development decision was made.

However, it is only when considered in hindsight that such studies are seen as important for software decisionmaking. In fact, only two of the programs studied (G and H) supported pre-RFP studies focused on computer resources; the remaining six program offices failed, at this point, to deal with software in an explicit fashion.

One conclusion could be that the SPO expects the contractor's proposal to "fill in the blanks" left in the software picture painted by the RFP. Indeed, in all eight cases, the defense contractor community had at least some, and often substantial, influence on the content of the development RFP. Air Force participants seem to manage according to the view that software requirements first emerge from cooperative efforts to prepare a development RFP, and that these efforts constitute the first step in the software-development process.

Activity 3: Formation of the Computer Resources Working Group (CRWG) and Preparation of a Draft Computer Resources Integrated Support Plan (CRISP) (see U.S. Air Force 1975, vol. 2). In most acquisitions, this activity is concurrent with RFP preparation. The objectives are to satisfy the requirement for an early draft of the plan and to create a computer resources focal point within the program office.

Air Force Regulation 800–14 (U.S. Air Force 1975) suggests (but does not require) the formation of a CRWG and requires the preparation of a support plan. However, throughout the 1970s there has been little recognition in official Air Force guidance that a software working group might be a useful tool for integrating the various managerial aspects of a complex embedded computational subsystem. One or two recent programs have come to independent decisions to create such a group, but such programs have usually elected to form a new group rather than broaden the responsibilities of the existing CRWG. The general absence of a software focal point can be interpreted in two ways: either the complexity of the software development task is not appreciated by program office decisionmakers, or it is expected that the initial CRWG would assume that role as it became necessary.

The group's initial focus is on preparing the support plan and not on its own potential integrative role. Initial working groups were formed in four out of the eight programs studied; two of the remaining four put one together after the software effort began to exhibit problems. In five of these six cases (A, B, C, G, and H), the groups focused on preparing and maintaining the plan and did not thereafter perform liaison for embedded software. Only three of the cases studied formed specialized groups to deal explicitly with software management and integration issues (one was directed to do so by higher headquarters). One would conclude that a broadly chartered software working group was not viewed as a high-priority need of the program office.

Activity 4: Preparation for, and Attendance at the System Design Review (SDO). The timing of this event is variable, but it usually occurs within one or two months after the development contract is awarded. It precedes any preliminary design reviews and allows the Air Force to review the contractor's planning documentation and his allocation of requirements to software before he begins a preliminary design.

U.S. Air Force Regulation 800–14 (1974) lists seven items relating to software that should be reviewed at the SDR. U.S. Air Force Military Standard 1521 (1976) contains a special section listing thirteen specific software issues that should be included in this review. It also notes that the review should precede the identification of computer program configuration items. In most programs, however, system-level reviews ignored software almost entirely, except for making sure that contractor documentation included plans for software testing and support. Thus, reviews aside, participants appear to view software requirements allocation as a prerequisite to the preliminary design phase of software development.

Activity 5: Preparation for, and Attendance at, the Software Preliminary Design Reviews (PDR's). These reviews are usually held within six months of contract award (after any system design reviews) to assess the contractor's preliminary software design. The timing and guidance associated with this review suggest that preliminary design is carried out between the system and the preliminary design reviews. Furthermore, the fact of a review at this point suggests a degree of flexibility in the reviewed software design. Theoretically, major portions of that design may, if necessary, be replaced by the products of new design efforts.

For five of the eight programs studied (A through D and F), the preliminary software reviews had little technical substance. This was true whether or not the program was of recent enough origin to be affected by new and more specific guidance. U.S. Air Force Military Standard 1521A (1976) mentions seventeen specifically reviewable items of information for computer program configuration items. Six examples of this large list are further highlighted in U.S. Air Force Regulation 800–14 (1975). For these programs, the reviews were focused on management issues. The people involved claim that, because of the shortage of technically qualified software personnel, reviews of management planning must act as proxy for substantive technical reviews. All eight program offices depended quite heavily on periodic technical-interchange meetings for maintaining some degree of technical oversight. One program manager noted that the software might be adequately reviewed using a combination of reviews and formalized interchange meetings, but this rarely occurred. The primary focus of the meetings appears to be the resolution of ''action items'' identified at the reviews, dealing mainly with inconsistencies in documentation or planning and only infrequently with technical questions.

Moreover, administrative pressures on acquisition schedules and budgets can act to discourage any but the most unassailable arguments for design reconsideration. Such pressures instead encourage pressing forward, and foster an attitude of ''we'll work it out later, when we know more.'' Systems A, C, and D provide the best examples of this characteristic. In A and C, software design and coding proceeded in the face of early and clear indicators that user requirements were poorly understood. It was not until formal testing began that serious consideration was given to redesigning the software—by then a quite expensive matter. Software development for system D was allowed to proceed despite strong suspicions that a crucial element of the software package was poorly conceived. The result of overriding those suspicions was a delay of one full year in system delivery.

With the exception of programs G and H, none of the program office personnel interviewed felt that a preliminary software review was likely to identify technical shortcomings not already caught by the contractor. Non-defense personnel were used in only three of the eight programs to technically augment the SPOs review team. The argument was that such review efforts were rarely useful in the past.

From these observations we can derive the postures summarized below. The last element of the list is derived from a trend developed over the last four activities.)

Preliminary software design is, for the most part, initiated and carried out during the first few months of the development contract.

The software design is, at preliminary review time, still quite flexible, changes resulting from a design review can be easily accommodated.

The software-development process is stepwise in nature; the outputs of each step provide most of the inputs required by the subsequent step. Once begun, it runs in parallel with other system acquisition activities.

Activity 6: Approval and Baselining of the Software Development Specifications. Generally this activity is one product of a preliminary design review; occasionally approval comes earlier than that. The objective is to establish agreement among all participants that the currently approved (baselined) design will be used to develop a more detailed design.

Outside of format and required subject matter—for which Military Standards 483 (1970) and 490 (1968) provide explicit guidance—a program office is on its own in evaluating the validity and consistency of a software specification. It must rely on the expertise and experience of its assigned personnel.

In seven of the eight programs, draft specifications were reviewed in a piecemeal fashion. As they evolved from very general to more specific and complex documents, the only parts reviewed were those that differed from the immediately preceding version. Once these differences were understood, the whole document was assumed to be understood. With this procedure, only inconsistencies apparent in the updated portions are likely to be noticed, while subtler and equally harmful anomalies— generated, for example, by increasingly complex relationships between newly updated and unmodified features—slip through the cracks to emerge later as quite apparent and very expensive problems.

Cases A through D either failed completely to baseline the software design, or did such a poor job of software engineering that the existence of a baseline configuration was immaterial. At this time, only three of the remaining cases (E, F, and H) have progressed far enough to illuminate the effects of a software baseline. Of these, two are being managed under contracts that waive delivery of finalized software documentation until late in the development cycle. For these programs, the software baseline established at the preliminary review relies on Air Force review of interim engineering documents, and a great deal of faith is placed in the contractor's competence and motivation. The third program relies on a documentation scheme composed, in part, of infrequently used but authorized formats and, in part, of program-unique requirements. The resulting scheme appears to be very effective thus far in controlling a complex software-engineering program; it has also avoided (so far) snowballing in volume and therefore in the time required for its review, update, and maintenance by program-office personnel.

In summary, this activity is conducted as though the managers believed that:

Design baselining follows preliminary design and precedes detailed design.

Technical skills become increasingly important to acquisition management as software development proceeds.

Given appropriate personnel, discretionary procedures can be superior to adherence to standards when complex programs are involved.

Activity 7: Initiate Configuration Management on Software Subsystem Development. This activity occurs after an allocated baseline for software has been approved, generally after the final software-development specifications have been approved. This activity is intended to control and document changes to the status of each major aspect of software development: requirements, design, implementation, and testing. U.S. Air Force Regulation 800–14 (1975) discusses both the need for, and some of the actions currently associated with, configuration management for computer programs; it augments the contents of Military Standards 483, 490, and 1521A and U.S. Air Force Regulation 65–3. Standard 483 also sets forth the required engineering change procedures for computer software and for the associated documentation products.

Personnel in three of the programs examined complained that the paperwork related to software configuration management consumed enough resources to substantially reduce their ability to mount a technically competent management effort. This was seen as less of a problem in the other five programs, each of which involved some deviation in format or delivery schedule from standard documentation practices. The most frequently observed deviation was a delay in the deliverable dates for finalized software specifications. In this context, "finalized" refers to a complete and formally produced document that is fully responsive to the format and subject-matter standards contained in existing government regulations. The implication here is that it is not necessary to require documentation in final format as input to formal reviews. It appears that, given competent personnel, reviews can be carried out in an acceptable fashion using interim engineering documents and notebooks that are only later finalized according to military-standard requirements. Indeed, the software staff in these five programs claimed that they were able to devote more time to technical issues as a direct result of the lower paperwork burden. However, these changes were two-edged. While increasing the time available for technical review, they also increased program office dependence on scarce software expertise and experience. For example, with formal software documentation deliverable later in the development life-cycle, detail that was customarily available in early test planning and configuration management documents was received much later in the process. This placed increased reliance on the knowledge and information brought to these tasks by individuals.

Regardless of the formal procedures used, without such resources software design anomalies are often not caught until visible cost growth and schedule slips occur. In program D, for example, the Air Force did not perceive the need for a schedule extension imposed by the approval of a particularly large software change. A breakdown in communications with the user then led to divergent assumptions about the system's operational characteristics and capabilities and to development delays needed to resolve the ensuing problems. Programs A and C had similar experiences.

In summary, configuration-management procedures cannot substitute for training and experience, and can hinder the best use of scarce personnel. Where good people are available, too much paperwork dilutes their ability to attend to technical issues. Where good people are absent, technical issues will be inadequately addressed regardless of the reporting procedures involved.

Activity 8: Preparation for, and Attendance at, the Software Critical Design Reviews (CDRs). These reviews are usually held three to four months after the preliminary reviews and are focused on the contractor's detailed, flowchart-level design for the software subsystem. Military Standard 1521A lists six specific items of documentation that should be given detailed review regarding each major software item. U.S. Air Force Regulation 800–14 (1975) expands the list to nine. Just as a preliminary design review precedes and guides the detailed design phase for software products, the critical review is expected to identify and approve the specific computer program documentation that is to guide coding and testing. Here, the regulation states explicitly that no actual programming should be done until the components of the entire software subsystem have passed a critical design review.

However, the handling of these reviews was quite erratic across the eight programs studied. Six of the eight reported them low in techical content, emphasizing instead management issues because the program offices were unable to field technically competent review teams. One program had no formal reviews, relying instead on informal meetings. Two others held reviews, but relied on informal meetings for most of their technical oversight. (Again, the formal reviews were skewed sharply toward managerial concerns.) One program lumped software reviews— both technical and managerial—into the system-level reviews. Another held reviews in all software categories except that of support. Support software was thought to be an off-the-shelf procurement, requiring no review. (Instead, it turned into a major unplanned development effort.) Still another program blamed the shallow technical content of its software reviews not on scarce expertise, but on a program office decision to allow the software specifications to float until software testing began and the resultant absence of a baseline against which to review.

By the time critical reviews for software get underway, program office software personnel appear to spend most of their time reviewing and approving contractor-supplied documentation, resolving action items raised during earlier reviews (or under other circumstances), and responding to the growing requirements of configuration management. Simply coping with the paperwork required by these activities takes an enormous amount of time. As a result, time is scarce for carefully evaluating the complex design and interface information that is crucial to identifying potential problems.

The two remaining programs (G and H) stand in sharp relief against the six just described. One developed, documented, and implemented explicit plans for each formal review and orchestrated the contractor's presentations to allow the review team maximum technical oversight. That team was itself augmented by several technically trained and experienced outside consultants. The other program enjoys the services of a well-trained and operationally experienced Air Force officer assigned as chief software engineer. This individual and his small team appear to have designed the software-engineering task to ''close the cracks'' through which errors fall in more traditional programs. This program is still in the early stages of development; it bears watching as a herald of more effective planning for software engineering.

Despite this recent evidence to the contrary, this activity suggests a management belief that:

The use of outside software expertise is not an effective tool for improving the effectiveness of software management.

Trained and experienced individuals are not absolutely required for effective software engineering management.

The Elements of a Model

In the following paragraphs, we use the characteristics identified above to derive a model of the software development process that is implicit in Air Force software management practices. With this objective in mind, we refined those characteristics and then examined them for obvious patterns and common themes. Table 4–2 shows the result in two specific categories: the ordered activities perceived by the Air Force as involved in the contractors' software development process, and the relationship of these activities to the full range of system acquisition events.

Ordered Activities

Software development is viewed as consisting of several distinct but interrelated activities, each subject to a certain degree of Air Force oversight. The process begins, as shown in table 4–2, with an analysis by the contractors that yields the basic system requirements to be satisfied by computer programs. The next steps are to generate preliminary software designs, document them, approve them as a baseline for future design evolution, and initiate certain controls on further changes. Detailed program design, once approved, is then followed by individual program development and checkout.

Table 4–2

Software-Development Characteristics Based on Acquisition Management Behavior

Ordered Activities
Software requirements emerge from efforts to prepare a development RFP; these efforts constitute the first steps in the software-development process.
Software preliminary design follows the allocation of software requirements and is carried out during the first part of the full-scale development phase.
Design baselining follows preliminary design and immediately precedes the detailed design phase.
Software detailed designs must be approved prior to coding release.
Programming and checkout begins after the critical design review.

Relationship to System Acquisition Events
The software life-cycle begins as system acquisition enters the full-scale development phase.
Software development runs parallel to, but is separate from, other aspects of the system-acquisition process.
The software development process is stepwise in nature; the outputs of each step provide most of the inputs for subsequent steps.
The software development process is initiated during and wholly contained within the system's full-scale development phase.

Relationship to System Acquisition Events

Implictly, Air Force program office software managers view software development as a process that begins with—and is wholly contained within—the full-scale development segment of the system acquisition life-cycle. Only then is an effort made to identify and acquire personnel with expertise focused on the computer resources embedded in the system. This means that all of the software management activities of the SPO are initiated and, for the most part, completed during that period of time (see figure 4–3). This includes those activities shown in table 4–2, plus others not studied here such as testing, integration, and so on.

Once begun, the software development process is seen as running in parallel with, but generally separate from, the majority of other contractor activities, most of which may be associated with some form of hardware development. There is a significant degree of parallelism both within the activities comprising the perceived software process and among them.

In addition to the characteristics highlighted above, table 4–3 shows a number of other descriptive variables that have been extracted from appendix A for each program. This table lends emphasis to certain issues already discussed and provides another perspective on the Air Force's software management process.

At this point, it is possible to construct a model of the software development process as implied by current acquisition management practice. Figure 4–4(a) presents a refinement of the Air Force acquisition

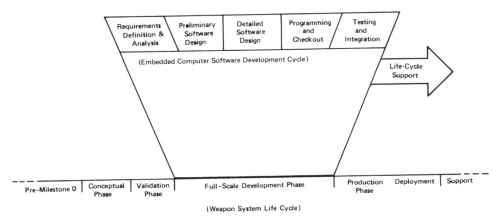

Figure 4–3. General Structure Implied by Management Activities

management model shown earlier as figure 4–1. Figure 4–4(b) shows the software-development model implicit in the model in figure 4–4(a). Thus we have a partial answer to one of the questions set earlier in this chapter: The Air Force is managing the process depicted in figure 4–4(b).

Figure 4–5 answers the second question: How does the process being managed (the model of figure 4–4[b]) relate to the model upon which official Air Force policy is based? The question is an important one, because it bears on the degree to which guidance is effective in complex and idiosyncratic management environments. The discussion will point to the major similarities and differences between existing guidance and observed practice. The issue will be reconsidered in more detail in a subsequent chapter.

Figure 4–5 compares the model contained in the Air Force regulation most relevant to software acquisition (U.S. Air Force 1975) with the model extracted from observed management practice (figure 4–4[b]). The figure also compares both to the overall system acquisition cycle. Two things seem apparent: the activities portrayed in both models as manageable components of the software-development process look quite similar, as does their ordering. When compared to the system acquisition cycle, however, there are some discrepancies. The text of U.S. Air Force Regulation 800–14 (1975) notes that the computer program development process may occur over more than one system acquisition phase, or that it may be contained within one phase (U.S. Air Force 1975, pp. 2–3). On the other hand, an accepted and widely quoted study of avionics software acquisition states that the beginning of the software life-cycle corresponds to the beginning of the system acquisition cycle (Logicon Corporation 1976). This discrepancy between system and software life-

Table 4–3
Summary of Software Acquisition Case Studies

System	DOD Software Management[a]	System Software Problems[b]	Program Initiation	SPO Formed	Explicit Software Attention	System Definition Contract	Software Focal-Point	External Consultants	Software Data Collected
A	1	0	1968	1968	Post-RFP[b]	No	No	No[d]	No
B	3	3	1965	1969	RFP	No	No	No	No
C	1	1	1971	1972	RFP	No	No	No[d]	No
D	2	1	1970	1972	RFP	No	No	No	No
E	4/5	3	1972	1974	Pre-RFP	Yes	Yes	Yes	Some
F	3	3	1974	1976	RFP	No	No	No	No
G	5[c]	5	1977	1977	Pre-RFP	Yes	Yes	Yes	No
H	5	4	1975	1977	Pre-RFP	Yes	Yes	Yes	Some

[a]Subjective evaluation: Software management. 0 = absent; 1 = poor; 2 = deficient; 3 = ambiguous; 4 = fair; 5 = good; 6 = excellent.

[b]Subjective evaluation: Problems. 0 = fundamental; 1 = major; 2 = significant; 3 = moderate; 4 = few; 5 = rare; 6 = none.

[c]Request for proposal for full-scale engineering development competition.

[d]Answer of "yes," late in program, in response to question regarding software problems.

[e]Software approach seems well-informed, but program in early stages.

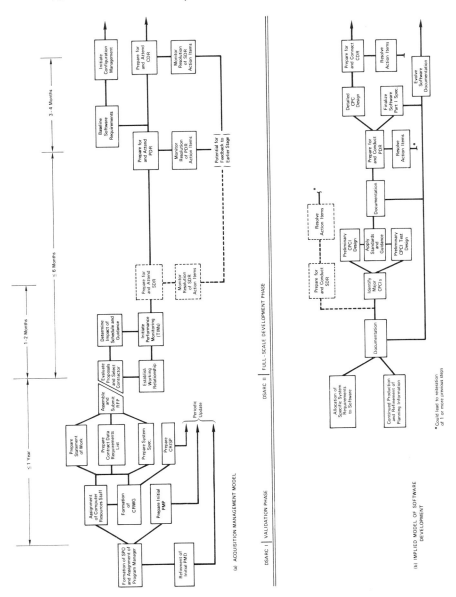

Figure 4–4. Software Development as Implied by Management Practice

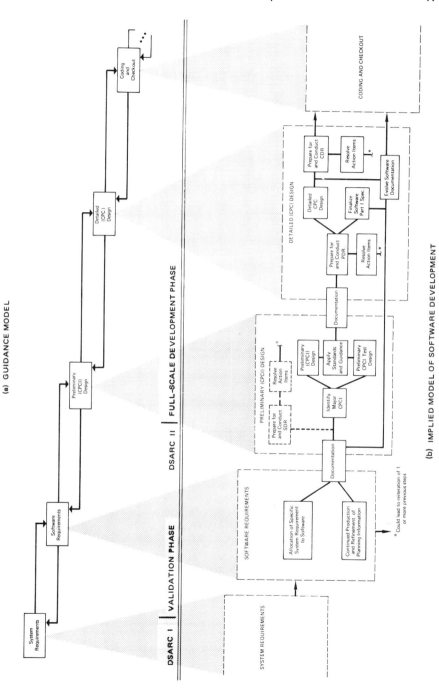

(a) GUIDANCE MODEL

(b) IMPLIED MODEL OF SOFTWARE DEVELOPMENT

Note: DSARC = Defense System Acquisition Review Committee

Figure 4–5. Software Development: Guidance Model versus Implicit Management Model

Table 4–4
Software Development Characteristics Based on Actual Development Programs

Ordered Activities

System definition studies lead to overall system requirements and to functional breakdowns for each anticipated subsystem.

Computer subsystem definition flows from system definition studies. Experimentation, simulation, vendor contacts, and other studies are used to develop and evaluate alternatives.

Preliminary software designs emerge gradually as a function of the evolution and analysis of subsystem requirements, acceptable designs, and coordination with other system and subsystem components.

Software design elaboration receives increasing attention as largely informal analyses and design decisions are reevaluated, documented, given formal status, and compiled into a technical proposal.

Detailed software designs begin to appear as work continues to extend and elaborate upon selected preliminary software designs.

Programming and checkout begins in many cases prior to official reviews, based on the contractor's perception of schedule variables and technical risks and on the level of design achieved in each case.

Relationship to System-Acquisition Events

The software life-cycle begins at the same time as the system acquisition life-cycle.

Software acquisition activities span the system-acquisition process.

Software development runs parallel to, and is largely integrated with, the development of certain other system components.

Although several stages are discernable, a high degree of interdependence, iteration, and change are the essential characteristics of software-development projects.

Table 4–5
Software Development Characteristics Based on Acquisition Management Behavior

Ordered Activities

Software requirements emerge from efforts to prepare a development RFP; these efforts constitute the first steps in the software-development process.

Software preliminary design follows the allocation of software requirements and is carried out during the first part of the full-scale development phase.

Design baselining follows preliminary design and immediately precedes the detailed design phase.

Software detailed designs must be approved prior to coding release.

Programming and checkout begins after the critical design review.

Relationship to System-Acquisition Events

The software life-cycle begins as system acquisition enters the full-scale development phase.

Software development runs parallel to, but is separate from, other aspects of the system acquisition process.

The software development process is stepwise in nature; the outputs of each step provide most of the inputs for subsequent steps.

The software development process is initiated during and wholly contained within the system's full-scale development phase.

cycles is evident in a large number of studies. In the present study, five of the eight programs examined were managed as though software development could not begin until the system itself reached full-scale development. In fact, when the characteristics that emerge from Air Force management behavior are compared in detail to those actually associated with contractor software development, a number of discrepancies emerge. (See tables 4–2 and 3–1, reproduced here for convenience (as tables 4–4 and 4–5.) Not only do the two views differ as to the activities involved in software development, but the relationship of each view to the system acquisition cycle is opened to question. The next chapter examines these discrepancies in more detail by comparing software development as implied by the Air Force's acquisition management behavior with the actual software development activities of contractors.

5 Comparative Analysis

Before we can proceed with the comparison, we must develop a framework for doing so. The framework will be derived from work on how organizations adapt to changes in their environments. That work was reviewed in chapter 2, and three diagnostic propositions, summarized below, were developed to guide the discussion in this chapter.

We saw in chapter 2 that one way organizations adapt is by making changes in their structure. There is agreement in the literature that organizations will be less effective to the extent these changes are slow in coming. Our first proposition states,

> The structure of large organizations is often slow to adapt to environmental change.

If the Air Force is slow to adapt, we might expect to find outmoded organizational structures applied to software acquisition management. This would be indicated, for example, if the Air Force management structure did not coincide with the basic structure of the software development life-cycle as actually carried out by vendors.

Closely related to structural changes are changes in an organization's operational processes; these also undergo change as adaptation proceeds. Here, again, a lack of timely response can lead to problems. Proposition two states,

> The processes of large organizations are often slow to adapt to environmental change.

Among other things, this suggests that management procedures may persist that do not address all of the important component activities of the software development process. This could appear, for example, as inconsistencies in the specific activities associated with software development in the models of different actors.

A third important aspect, recently reemphasized in the theoretical literature, is the influence of attentional mechanisms on adaptation. The idea is that organizations attend only to those parts of the environment that are perceived as relevant to their operations. This implies that organizations cannot adapt to newly relevant, but unperceived, environmental conditions. Thus, unless the Air Force has developed procedures for timely access to and use of information relevant to software, it may not perceive when adaptation is needed. Our third proposition, therefore, states

> Attentional and informational mechanisms are central to an organization's ability to adapt to environmental change.

These propositions lead to three specific questions about the conduct of acquisition management for embedded software.

1. Does the structure of the Air Force's acquisition management organization adequately reflect the basic structure of the software development life-cycle?
2. Does the Air Force's acquisition management organization adequately address the key activities associated with actual software development?
3. Does the Air Force's acquisition management organization perceive and make effective use of available information related to software?

Analysis

Figure 5–1 will act as a conceptual anchor. It summarizes the main features of each model in terms of the descriptive categories used in chapters 3 and 4: ordered activities and their relationship to the system acquisition life-cycle. Figure 5–1(a) shows the software development process as implied by Air Force management practices; figure 5–1(b) shows the true development process as observed in the actions of software contractors. It is clear that there are real differences between the two models.

Following the framework, we first examine how well the Air Force model represents the basic structure of the true model. As shown in figure 5–1(b), software development is structured in much the same way as overall system development. Software moves through several somewhat overlapping but nonetheless distinct stages. Each stage involves certain key activities and each calls for somewhat different skills and resources. In the needs-analysis stage, for example, inputs from ongoing research and development in software (and other) technologies combine with inputs from the earliest wide-ranging discussions about system function and performance to give an overall direction to the software development effort. As we saw in chapter 4, decisions at this point on system parameters—weight limits, electrical power characteristics, and the like—lead

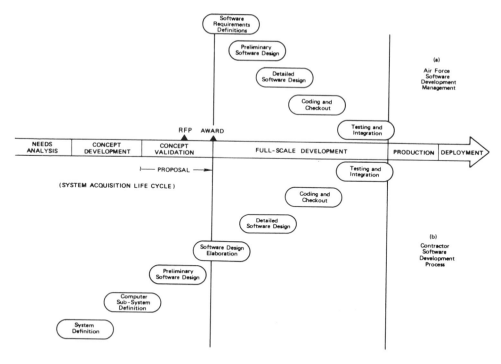

Figure 5–1. Two Models of Software Development

to certain constraints on the computer hardware to be carried by the system. In turn, such constraints influence the nature and performance potential of the associated software. For example, memory cycle time can dramatically influence the design of software that must perform and coordinate a wide range of real-time functions. Decisions at this stage are usually made by specialized groups composed primarily of senior engineering-management personnel. They are supported by studies whose primary focus is on system performance, and coordinated with senior representatives from the Air Force's developing, supporting, and using organizations.

By contrast, development-stage activities are more narrowly focused on issues of computer program design and implementation. This stage implements decisions from earlier stages. The groups involved still specialize, but are more often composed of middle-level technicians, unit engineers, and programmers. The point is that each stage has somewhat different objectives and requires different skills, facilities, and (often) organizational principles from other stages. Contractors have long recognized this basic structuring: it is reflected in their approach to management. There is a specific organization of personnel and facilities for each major stage. In some cases, these are separate organizational entities, but they need not be. The same basic set of resources can address each stage in sequence, adding or subtracting specific characteristics and skills along the way so as to tailor the organization to the tasks at hand. Some contractors argue that this is the preferred approach, given the iterative nature of, and feedback among, the different stages.

By comparison, the Air Force model at figure 5–1(a) assumes that software development must wait until certain aspects of the overall system have been decided upon, which decisions then supply the basic information required for designing and implementing computer programs. This model has less descriptive relevance for embedded software development than for, say, an airframe assembly line, wherein step B cannot begin until step A has been completed. The comparison seems particularly apt if one agrees that the management practices currently applied to software originated in, and are more relevant to, an era when hardware was the predominant concern in system acquisition.

The Air Force model reflects an organizational structure that considers the software acquisition cycle as accomplished wholly within a single stage of system acquisition. The implication is that only after system function, performance, and other specifications have been formally documented and accepted can detailed attention be given to software for that system. In fact, as discussed in chapter 3, the Air Force defers explicit attention to software acquisition until just before the system enters the full-scale development stage. By that time (as is evident from figure 5–1[b]), the contractor's software development process has been underway for some time—often for as long as one to two years—and prior decisions constrain the choices and opportunities facing the newly formed software management organization.

The approach in figure 5–1(a) has its roots in an earlier time when, in fact, it was reasonably effective for managing software acquisition. As we saw in chapter 1, digital technology found its way only gradually, at first, into defense systems. For a time, it did not matter whether or not the customer paid close attention to the software associated with this technology. It was provided by contractors where it was required and was neither technically nor managerially as complex as it is now. The use of software to perform certain limited functions was novel, but it did not appear to require management practices different from those already in place and tuned to hardware-intensive acquisitions.

Very few anticipated the shockingly rapid growth that has occurred over the past twenty years in the complexity, applicability, and use of software technology (recall figure 1–1). The result is that today's embedded software environment is radically different from that of the 1960s, and the speed with which this difference has come about has led to problems for complex organizations whose adaptation machinery moves at a slower pace. The failure of software acquisition management to represent activities that occur before the full-scale development phase reflects just such problems. The organizational structure that currently determines acquisition management practices is more in tune with the software environment of the mid-1960s than with that of the early 1980s. In other words, software acquisition for modern embedded computers is managed by an organizational structure that has not kept pace with changes in the environment to which it must respond. This outmoded structure does not give adequate attention to all of the relevant stages of the software acquisition process.

Another way in which the models of figure 5–1 differ is in how they represent the key activities associated with software development. Table 5–1 brings together the key activities for each model. On the left are listed the activities managed by the Air Force; on the right are the activities contractors actually engage in to produce software. Several differences are apparent. First, only four activities are common to both models (preliminary design, detailed design, coding and checkout, and integration and testing). Second, there are two activities in the contractor model (system definition and design elaboration) that seem to have no counterpart in the Air Force model. Finally, there are differences in the implementation of the activities and in their relationship to certain stages of the system acquisition life-cycle.

Mission needs—and therefore requirements—typically change during the acquisition period. Moreover, any approach incorporates compromises determined by constraints on available technologies, budgets, and other resources. Thus, a given set of requirements frequently satisfies a constrained version of the original mission need. One of the activities not represented in the Air Force model is that of system definition, which assesses the degree to which mission requirements are met by alternative

Table 5–1
Comparison of Key Software Development Activities

Air Force Version	*Contractor Version*
1. Software requirements definition and analysis	1. System definition
2. Preliminary software design	2. Definition of computational sub-system
3. Detailed software design	3. Preliminary software design
4. Coding and checkout	4. Software design elaboration
5. Integration and testing	5. Initiation of programming
	6. Detailed software design
	7. Continuation of coding and checkout
	8. Integration and testing

conceptualizations of the system. This task is, as the name implies, concerned with the overall function of the system. It is among the very first considerations in the evolution of an acquisition program. The decision-making environment emphasizes primary mission characteristics—for example, the ecological charcteristics such as terrain, weather, and so on, and the threat environment as revealed by counterforce technology and so on. As the alternatives are examined, attention focuses on things like system performance and structural variables. For an aircraft, the former would include speed, range, ceiling, and weaponry; the latter, size, weight, and overall configuration. Decisions made at this time about these variables direct the expenditure of millions, perhaps billions, of dollars over the ensuing eight- to eleven-year acquisition period and the subsequent operational lifetime of a system.

The Air Force apparently fails to perceive the importance of system definition to software development. So invisible is the relationship that none of the Air Force personnel interviewed during this study could remember any substantive concern for software during their participation in system definition tasks.

The contractor, however, knows that system definition initiates the software acquisition cycle. What is crucial from the software perspective is that very real boundaries are placed on the design of its component subsystems as a system is defined. The spaces in an airframe assigned to avionics devices, for example, constrain the viable computer hardware alternatives. In turn, certain important software design issues are virtually decided by hardware characteristics like processing speed, storage capacity, and communications bandwidth. What will not fit cannot be considered in later subsystem designs unless the customer approves costly structural modifications to a system design to which he may already be committed. The evolving output of the system definition effort, in turn, provides primary inputs for defining the computational subsystem; these can place inadvertent constraints on its design as well.

The process of developing a proposal, submitting it to the Air Force, and refining it during source selection comprise another unrepresented, but important—and conceptually separable—aspect of the software effort. During this period—the design elaboration phase—several things are done that set the stage for future activities. Software documentation (primarily engineering notes and internal study documents) are consolidated, reviewed, and reproduced in proposal format. In so doing, many heretofore informal ideas and decision about preliminary software design—for example, interface design and specific software functions—are refined and given formal status in the initial proposal.

The design-elaboration phase is also used to finish and document studies and experiments whose major results have already influenced the proposal and that may be described during later reviews.

The resulting formalization, refinement, and documentation of preliminary software designs lends validity and conviction to the contractor's software efforts up to this point. For the contractor, it represents a staging point between his preliminary design efforts and the next major software engineering task: detailed design. Parts of the contractor's software project may actually begin to move into the detailed design stage prior to the award of the development contract. By their nature, all these separate activities constitute an elaboration of—and formal commitment to—the software design and engineering decisions that have evolved to this point in the contractor's software effort.

The lack of representation of these two activities in the Air Force model demonstrates an inadequacy in the set of management procedures it has applied to software acquisition. In other words, two activities that are key parts of actual software development practice are unrepresented in the Air Force's management procedures.

Another difference between the two models relates to the processes and timing associated with preliminary requirements and design work. The Air Force model represents software requirements definition and preliminary design as separate and consecutive phases, both of which occur after the award of the development contract. What is actually observed is that software requirements and initial design emerge from a contractor's earliest system definition efforts. These activities predate the development contract (by one to two years, in some cases).

This is hardly surprising; as noted earlier, contractors try to learn as much as possible about subsystem development while developing their proposals. To estimate and submit cost and schedule information, they develop and examine alternative designs both for the system as a whole and for its major subsystems. Where software is concerned, questions of design are difficult to avoid once requirements are under discussion. Identifying the major requirements of a computational subsystem forces attention to the major computer program configuration items as well as to their structural and logical relationships with one another. Each major configuration item embodies a coherent group of software requirements; the extent to which these requirements are met is sensitive to module interfaces and other design issues. The ensuing interative testing, simulations, studies of past systems, and examination of new techniques produces a great deal of information relevant to software design. Contractors develop and use this information, but may not include it all in their proposals.

In summary, the Air Force model has the following characteristics:

It represents reasonably well the last portion of the actual software development cycle.

It misrepresents several activities in both substance and timing.

It fails completely to account for two critical steps.

Since this model reflects how the Air Force is organized for managing software acquisition, we can conclude that the organization does not adequately represent the key activities associated with software development.

The Air Force and contractor community maintain an essentially continuous dialog regarding new developments of potential military significance. Topics related to software are not intentionally excluded from this dialog; however, such interchanges typically involve—for the Air Force—individuals who are concerned primarily with when and how well the system as a whole will perform its mission. To such people, implementation details such as the development of software have been of secondary importance. Since a contractor will obviously tailor his presentations to the biases of his audience, software is rarely given explicit attention during this time; rather, its effects are given in terms of performance.

We have seen that software is crucial (1) to the overall success of the acquisition program itself, (2) to mission performance, and (3) to the deployed system's adaptivity to new and modified requirements. We must therefore question why attention to software is deferred until the start of the development phase. As suggested earlier, part of the answer lies in the use of acquisition machinery that is still organized to meet the software environment of a decade or more ago. Thus, before we can expect significantly improved organizational adaptation, the Air Force must modify its perception of that environment to reflect a 1980s world. Furthermore, given the speed with which this technology advances, facilities for regularly updating that perception are also needed.

As we saw in chapter 2, recent adaptation research suggests that unperceived environmental variables cannot contribute information that sensitizes an organization to new requirements for adaptation. Without such information, we would expect adaptive measures to be evoked by encountered problems and to reflect piecemeal solutions to those problems rather than a more comprehensive approach. Current attempts by the Air Force to solve its software acquisition problems are consistent with this view. Given that much potentially useful information exists, it seems reasonable to conclude that the Air Force's attentional mechanisms often fail to make useful information available for acquisition managers.

Summary

This chapter has argued that many of the Air Force's problems in acquiring embedded software are rooted in organizational structures and processes that are inappropriate to actual software development practice. These kinds of problems persist, it is further argued, because the Air Force has yet to pay adequate (that is, explicit and timely) attention to information that could both alert the organization to new indicators of needed change and suggest what those changes should be.

The next chapter discusses the implications of this argument for new or updated Air Force policy, examines impediments to such changes, and discusses the incentives that led one recent program to overcome some of those impediments and improve the outcome of its software development process.

6 Impediments and Incentives

The Air Force's problems with embedded software are neither recent nor unique. In fact, most major software acquisition programs, whether defense or non-defense, risk problems of the same sort: delays, cost growth, and deficient performance. Depending upon the prominence of software in a product—or upon the user's dependence on software performance— these problems can have a large or comparatively small overall impact.

In the last fifteen years, the Air Force has moved from very limited, introductory use of embedded software to a position in which software can determine the operational effectiveness of a computer-based system. Acquisition problems have grown more important along with this increased dependence on software.

The task of increasing the software literacy of the Air Force has been underway for years through various studies, workshops, and laboratory programs. The Air Force continually monitors programs, evaluates studies, and makes incremental changes to policy in an effort to stay on top of a set of very dynamic technologies. At the present time, however, these efforts have had their major influence on a relatively small number of directly involved individuals. The lessons have not yet filtered upward with the necessary force and clarity to the levels of management that can respond to them by changing the overall structure of the acquisition management organization. Furthermore, given the critical nature of defense software, the resultant emphasis on reliability, the increasingly complex operational requirements, and the extreme rapidity with which all these characteristics have come to dominate the software scene, it is not surprising that efforts to improve software outcomes often yield inadequate results.

The Air Force's management of software acquisition has been described as outmoded, and it is suggested that this characteristic is a primary contributor to software problems in modern systems. The analysis in chapter 5 points to some clear-cut changes to existing acquisition policy as it pertains to embedded software. We would expect outcomes to improve if, for example, the relevant Air Force organizations were restructured so as to encourage a more substantive concern for software earlier in the system acquisition decision path—treating software as a decision variable at the conceptual stage, as hardware is now. Such a structural change would, by implication, be supported by new procedures that would encourage management attention to all of the key development activities undertaken by defense contractors.

Simply pointing out organizational problems, however, does not automatically ease them; it would be naive to suggest that the required changes could be accomplished by rewriting Air Force policy documents. An intermediate step is necessary; one must undersand the factors giving rise to the problems and the pressures that tend to maintain them.

The Evolution of the Problem

When software was first introduced into defense systems, it was not accompanied by a phalanx of appropriately trained technicians and managers. Virtually all the personnel involved were hardware-oriented in perception, organization, and working procedures. It mattered little that software was underrepresented in the general scheme—software was a small part of the whole, and the problems it presented were also small. These days, software is still underrepresented in the perceptions, organization, and procedures of acquisition management personnel—but not in the systems they manage. The interviews and analyses conducted during this study suggest that the failure to appropriately develop and employ existing personnel and information is the most important factor giving rise to—and maintaining—current organizational problems.

It is important to understand that most of the issues discussed below also apply to other technical specialties. However, because software is of comparatively recent importance, there has been less time to generate the required personnel skills and diffuse them throughout the Air Force. Not only are there few people with enough training and experience to do the job, but the job itself—the evaluation of in-progress software development—is currently not well understood. Moreover, the software field is still expanding very rapidly, placing additional strains on training. Unlike skills in more mature technologies, five-year-old software skills border on obsolescence.

Personnel Development

As with any other discipline, software management requires personnel whose skills, training, and experience are specialized to the task. In the Air Force, there are a number of strong disincentives to such specialization that act in combination both to encourage the existing approach to software acquisition management and to deemphasize a perception that software is now a major influence on the system acquisition environment. Another major effect is to depress the supply of individuals who could, as they rise in rank and position, form the nucleus of a generation of decision makers with first-hand understanding of the potentials and problems of software technology. The primary disencentives are discussed in subsequent paragraphs.

As presently organized, the Air Force applies technical management skills to software primarily while a system program office exists (see figure 3–3). For most major programs, this is a period of about five years. Typically, program office personnel working on software-oriented tasks do so for a tour of duty that rarely exceeds three years; they are then reassigned to a new job that may not be closely related to their prior assignment. This practice has certain negative effects on software acquisition managment. In the first place, the temporary nature of assignments discourages innovation and, therefore, encourages the maintenance of existing techniques despite the best intentions of the people involved. Many of those interviewed mentioned a reluctance to propose new and potentially risky approaches because (1) they might easily be reassigned before their ideas reached fruition, thereby transferring much of the credit for a successful implementation to their replacement; and (2) any negative consequences could reflect badly on their competence and lead to less than favorable performance evaluations. For those individuals who are assigned to a SPO as replacements for the initial cadre, a significant part of their tour of duty may be devoted to maintaining the directions set by their predecessors while they learn the ropes and develop confidence in their new jobs. Once they have settled in, these personnel will tend to be motivated by the attitudes described earlier.

Moreover, individuals who perceive their software management job as temporary and who face possible reassignment to an entirely different job are rarely motivated to invest heavily in learning. Coupled with the tendency toward hands-off contractor relations—caused primarily by a chronic shortage in program office software skills—this inhibits the development of excellence in software management and maintains a certain organic mediocrity in those skills.

Another important disincentive is the fact that the Air Force has no formal career path for software managers. This may seem surprising, given at least a decade of serious concern for the adequacy of Air Force efforts in this area. On the other hand, the speed with which software has come to play such a crucial role in systems has worked against the development of such adaptive responses. Even if unremarkable, however, the absence of such a career path has detrimental consequences.

One such consequence is that professionalism in the software area is deemphasized. Most of the program offices examined approached the problem of staffing and planning for software acquisition management in an ad hoc fashion. Initial staff were typically drawn from available personnel, whether or not their experience and training were well-matched to the job. It was only where program directors had earlier experience with software problems that more careful initial staffing was accomplished. In other cases, such care was motivated by the need to recover from problems that, in hindsight, might have been prevented by careful staffing in initial stages.

Another consequence is to strengthen an already strong perception that specialization in software-intensive activities is a dead-end career choice for Air Force officers. To most of those interviewed, this perception reflected a more general attitude that specialization in any area besides flying and general business management runs counter to a successful Air Force career. (This does not include the comparatively few professional specialities like physician, attorney, chaplain, and so on that are encouraged.) Aversion to becoming known as a "software specialist" was evident in many of those interviewed, particularly among career-oriented officers.

These disincentives tend to select out of the Air Force those officers who have the strongest interests in software science, thereby hindering the upward diffusion of informed concern for software matters. The overall effect is to slow the growth of technical sophistication at organizational levels where policy decisions are made. Furthermore, since those who leave are more often than not young, recently trained, and technologically current, those who stay and eventually reach influential positions tend to be lower on the software learning curve and require more preparation in advance of decision making. Clearly, poorly informed decisions can result when time is short, and the earlier the decision making involved, the greater the potential for major consequences (see, for example, systems C and D, appendix A). This view also helps to explain the frequent tutorial nature of software design reviews and the often reported lack of substantive technical questioning by the Air Force review teams.

Although program directors who are sensitive to the influence of software may clearly perceive these problems, they have very limited means for combatting them. In the first place, program directors are in an unfavorable bargaining position in terms of offering opportunities to skilled personnel. They cannot compete with salaries offered by civilian firms that actively recruit personnel with software skills, and they cannot—except in rare instances—offer guaranteed promotions in military rank. It is possible, on the other hand, to assign an individual to a more prestigious position within the program office and to intercede on his behalf—through written and oral performance reviews—for promotion opportunities. However, to the extent these benefits are also available elsewhere, they are comparatively weak substitutes for more direct economic incentives. Moreover, the success associated with such efforts is proportional to the priority of the acquisition program in question; defense systems of high priority compete more successfully in these areas than do those of lesser influence. Very few programs and correspondingly few knowledgeable people enjoy such advantages. The incentives they offer are rarely available to the majority of those employed in software-intensive tasks.

Considered together, these things make it hard to imagine an environment less conducive to the effective development and use of software talent. The lack of incentives to learn and to specialize in software-related assignments discourages the development of management skills and contributes to a worsening skill retention problem. The relatively few highly skilled and motivated people that remain cannot provide the excellence needed by all programs. This situation keeps high-level Air Force attention focused on the optimal staffing of critical individual programs and hinders progress in adapting to the software environment as a whole. One result is a tendency to continue incremental tinkering with existing management practices without addressing more fundamental organizational issues. Another consequence is to effectively damp the speed with which a sophisticated grasp of software's influence reaches higher levels of Air Force management. Given the speed with which the technology generates new uses for computers, this tends to maintain an already unacceptable gap between software technology and the Air Force's ability to perceive and manage its most cost-effective and operationally relevant employment. In turn, dependence on software contractors is encouraged and, again, existing organizational structures and procedures tend to be maintained.

Obviously, there are exceptions to such general trends; one example is discussed in the last section of this chapter. However, the majority of programs examined in this study exhibit some or all of the characteristics described above.

Information Development

In view of this personnel environment, the ambiguity surrounding the development and use of software-related information—discussed in chapter 3—is not surprising. A number of theorists agree that organizations develop and use information primarily from environmental components perceived as important to organizational objectives (see especially Pfeffer and Salancik (1978) and Jackson and Morgan (1978). The picture that emerges from this study reveals a very uneven perception of software's importance to Air Force objectives. There is, for instance, a high sensitivity to the need for more and better information about all aspects of software technology at organizational levels concerned directly with acquiring, supporting, and employing systems with embedded computers. Especially in recent years, various conferences and workshops involving these organizations have emphasized this need.

At higher organizational levels, this emphasis is comparatively weaker. This is due, in part, to the increasing number of variables that must be factored into decision making at higher levels. Attention is fragmented; not all factors can receive equal consideration; one must set priorities. Some of those interviewed also pointed out that one tends to give priority to the most familiar factors of a problem. A long history of attention to hardware-mediated performance variables has given the Air Force a clear grasp of the importance of hardware characteristics to mission objectives. The current cadre of decision makers have grown up with, and contributed to, this environment. There is comparatively less familiarity with software influences at the policymaking level, suggesting that they receive a correspondingly lower priority. Thus, there is in the Air Force a range of sensitivities to the influence and importance of embedded software. This is to be expected in a complex organization undergoing technological reorientation more rapidly than anticipated.

Certain cross-cutting observations, however, do seem surprising. After allowing for the above-mentioned disincentives, there are still a good number of individuals at various locations and levels in the Air Force who are knowledgeable about software or are becoming so. These individuals, who represent the vanguard of that service's attempt to come to grips with the software problem, call frequent attention to the paucity of data upon which they base their decisions. It appears that poor use is made of existing and potentially rich sources of relevant information, either because Air Force decisionmakers fail to perceive its existence and relevance or because the cost of making such information available is seen as too high.

Two of the richest information sources for new program offices are the experiences of earlier programs and the decision making information developed for, but seldom completely revealed in, proposals from the defense-contractor community. Personnel interviewed in all but three of the programs examined in this study emphasized that project outcomes would be improved were this information effectively employed. The other three programs demonstrated the soundness of this suggestion (an example is discussed in the last section of this chapter).

Arguments against drawing on the experiences of earlier programs most often rest on claims that the systems under development are too different and that, in any event, personnel rotation and retirement often make the most relevant sources inaccessible to current programs. The second problem does exist to some extent, but there is little empirical evidence in support of the first. Barring extreme cases, neither software management techniques nor symptoms of problems seem to change very much as a direct result of differences in the specific functions of software developed for different systems. This comes clearly out of the analysis in chapter 4 (see also Glaseman and Davis 1980), and suggests that a lack of incentive, rather than technical impediments, underlies most of the resistance to learning from earlier programs. This view is consistent with arguments made previously and also with comments made by software management personnel in several of the program offices examined. Apparently program offices begin to respond very early to anticipated budget and schedule pressures. This tends to focus attention on the new system to the frequent exclusion of certain of its similarities to earlier systems—notably in management experiences. Program-office personnel view their rewards as based on achieving the cost and schedule objectives set forth early in contract negotiations. There is little incentive to focus attention on any management aspect of an earlier program that does not obviously shorten the time required to design, code, or test a specific piece of software.

Contractors, by contrast, develop a wealth of information on the design, implementation, testing, and associated costs of software as necessary input to a competitive development proposal. This study found that the software cost and schedule information contained in a proposal was most frequently used only in comparisons with other proposals at source-selection time; it was rarely examined to see if it was reasonable with respect to the technical effort proposed. This supports the contention, expressed at the 1980 Air Force Armament and Avionics Planning Conference, that the contractor's software competence is not regularly evaluated during the source-selection process. Another important issue is that much contractor-generated information in the form of, for example, experimental results, studies, early software design alternatives, engineering notes, and decision criteria, does not find its way to the Air Force in time to influence decision making. Proposals have typically devoted relatively few pages to software, presenting only a few results of what may easily represent one to two years of documented study. The potential utility of such information to conceptual-stage discussions—those taking place well before an RFP is developed—seems hard to overestimate. The Air

Force, however, is neither organized nor staffed to take advantage of this information. Other possible sources of useful information include the outputs of certain Air Force laboratories, such as Rome Air Development Center and the Wright Avionics Laboratory. An examination of these and other sources was beyond the resources of the present study.

To summarize: There appear to be pressures that maintain outmoded organizational structures and inadequate operating procedures for managing software acquisition. These pressures also direct attention away from existing information that could more effectively illuminate the software environment and perhaps lead to certain adaptive responses. This view suggests that matters would be improved if Air Force policymakers took steps to develop a more informed grasp of software technology and its various influences on defense systems. However, this kind of change takes time, and there is little evidence that the process can be significantly speeded up by paper analyses. The implementation and subsequent retraction of the recommendations of the 1976 Computer Resources Management Study (Drezner 1976) bears testimony to the uncertainties of this approach. What is needed is a clear demonstration that a change in organizational approach can improve project outcome and mission performance for specific, identifiable acquisition programs. We turn, therefore, to discuss a recent program in which nonstandard organizational factors reduced some of the problems mentioned earlier and thereby improved the program's outcome.

An Example

Due as much to unique circumstances as to explicit planning, program E (see appendix A) embodied certain departures in software-management practices from earlier acquisition programs. Because it was started as a prototype demonstration program, a small program office organization was formed much earlier than usual (two years before the RFP) to work with the contractors and guarantee relevance to Air Force interests. This "mini-SPO," as it was called, was also technically strong and participated in the system definition studies undertaken by what turned out to be program E's prime contractor. This participation persisted at both the technical and managerial levels throughout the years during which program E moved from a demonstration program to a system-acquisition program. This led to an earlier awareness of, and emphasis on, software characteristics that influenced alternative system concepts. Thus, in this case the SPOs activities exhibited closer than usual conformity to the overall structure of the contractor's software development process.

Furthermore, by becoming involved at the system definition stage and continuing its participation, the program office was able to apply some degree of management oversight to more of the key activities involved in software development, some of which (as was shown in chapters 4 and 5) typically occur well before the Air Force usually initiates formal software management tasks. Thus, a more appropriate organizational structure enabled more effective management by forcing attention to software-relevant organizational processes heretofore ignored.

However, the situation should not be exaggerated. The mini-SPO was not staffed explicitly for software expertise; the predevelopment benefits described above came about by a fortuitous combination of skilled, highly motivated contractors and experienced, well-organized Air Force personnel. In fact, most of the software management potential built up during this time was unrealized in the full-scale development program office (see appendix A). However, the program, being high in priority, had high visibility at the top policymaking levels of the Air Force. This led to concern at those levels that software not become a bottleneck, and external consultants were assigned to review the approach taken to software by both program office and contractor.

The result has been an unusually well-organized program office, better equipped—after an initial period of uncertainty—to take advantage both of a technically competent software staff and of the software information developed earlier by the mini-SPO. Even so, certain problems occurred that affected software costs and development schedules, though in a minor way. Such problems indicate the strength with which the Air Force organization resists even relatively minor changes to established procedures.

The history of the project to date shows that effective, though unplanned, manipulation of organizational variables at the program-office level can yield a good outcome. It is also significant that many of the changes came about because attention was paid to software at high policymaking levels. This suggests the potential benefits of more realistic perceptions of software's influence on the overall outcome of a program.

Summary

Outmoded organizational structures and operating procedures have been traced to problems in the access to and use of personnel and information. Adaptive behavior is hindered by long-standing personnel policies that discourage innovative management, learning, and specialization in the software area and, by the same token, encourage attrition in exactly those individuals most likely to raise the level of software literacy at policymaking levels in the Air Force. Moreover, existing sources of useful information remain untapped and so cannot contribute to improving the outcome of specific programs or to developing a more effective stance toward the software problem as a whole.

Taken together, these forces tend to maintain existing approaches to software acquisition management, along with the problems that go with them. However, several recent programs have demonstrated the benefits of rather fundamental—albeit limited—changes in the organization of software management. Many readers will observe that large software development projects in other sectors often experience the same kinds of problems faced by the Air Force; see, for example, Lehman (1979) and Head (1981). Moreover, where there have been clear successes in those other environments, at least partial credit is given to novel organizational modes and to explicit attention to new (or newly available) information. Thus, although the recommendations in the next chapter are intended for the Air Force, they are also relevant to a more general audience.

7 Policy Recommendations

We can view program E as a natural experiment in the use of organizational adaptation to improve the outcome of a software development project. The fact that software has been less troublesome for this program suggests that there is at least some potential for improvement within the framework of current organizational perceptions and policies. Other programs (programs G and H, in particular) have also reaped benefits from somewhat more limited organizational modifications. However, the fact that programs continue to encounter software-related difficulties despite such precautions suggests that the Air Force needs to improve its ability to apply collectively what it learns in individual cases. This, in turn, indicates a need to adapt the framework itself—that is, to develop and implement policy initiatives that, by requiring certain behaviors in all system acquisitions, encourage regular attention to important activities presently outside the purview of most software management structures.

Generally speaking, the analyses presented in earlier chapters suggest that the outcome of Air Force software projects can be improved by

1. Devoting earlier attention to software as a system-level decision variable.
2. Improving the empirical basis for decision making involved with software.
3. Making more effective use of existing personnel who are knowledgeable in the fields of computers and computer software.

The specific recommendations discussed below represent one possible approach to these goals. If they are implemented and the results evaluated, new information and additional insights should lead to improved techniques that are both relevant in the near term and more easily adapted to future changes. Different combinations of measures might be proposed by others. I would emphasize, however, that any successful approach must deal with the concerns identified in this research.

A number of recent programs have anticipated some of these recommendations; others come from the connections made in this study between organizational adaptation and the existing Air Force management model. None of them is problem free; some are controversial; but all represent actions that can be initiated now with a reasonable expectation of positive results. To wait for a less uncertain future is, to me, fruitless.

Recommendations

1. *Institute, during the conceptual stage of system acquisition, a formal organization with responsibility for developing and communicating alternative concepts for the role of software technology.*

During the concept development and validation stages, this group would reconcile emerging function, performance, testing, and support concepts with currently available software capabilities (recommending pertinent studies where necessary) and outline the expected advantages and disadvantages of alternative software implementations. Obviously, this group would require informational support from the contractor community, and this could pose problems, which are discussed later.

Such an organization might consist, at first, of a single individual. Several programs examined in the present study bear testimony to the major role played by single individuals in the ultimate success of a software acquisition. Program G is a good example of this point—see appendix A. However staffed, this group should be required to document its work so as to minimize the effects of personnel transfers that are bound to occur during the acquisition cycle. Moreover, documentation should be informal but guided by a standard format. Such a format should not be the object of prolonged study—rather, it should be allowed to evolve from initial suggestions based on informed judgment.

As the program moves into the full-scale development phase—the point at which present procedures call for the formation of a program office—this group would evolve into a software focal point for that office, bringing with it experience and documentation unavailable within the existing organizational structure. The intended role of such a focal point is exemplified in program E, in which that group provided an influential organizational superstructure for the computer resources working group and for other subgroups, each concerned with a different, but related, aspect of the software management task.

The major advantage of this recommendation is that it generates a better structural match between the Air Force's acquisition organization and the realities of a software development project. Additional benefits would accrue if this more formal approach early in the acquisition cycle lead to improved organizational learning and generated a better appreciation for software influences among high-ranking Air Force policymakers involved at that time. Those programs (E, G, and H) that, by accident or design, initiated attention to software well before the development contract was awarded were more successful in software development than the others were.

The disadvantages of this recommendation—besides the aforementioned difficulty in obtaining useful information from contractors—include locating and committing appropriate personnel and increasing the already heavy burden of paperwork. Although these problems will be addressed to some extent in later recommendations, immediate action based on the best available resources is needed. The personnel problem, for example, will not be solved in the foreseeable future, nor will contractors willingly release competitively sensitive information. Nevertheless, improvement must be sought in each area, and any positive step will represent progress.

2. *Require a formal and competitive system definition phase dealing explicitly with computer resources before an RFP for full-scale engineering development is sent out for bids.*

It appears from this and an earlier study that a formal system definition contract had a significant positive influence wherever it was used. It has been argued that the decisions associated with system definition are crucial for software development. It is significant that, of the programs examined, only the three more successful ones (programs E, G, and H) employed system-definition contracts. A formalization of both this process and its connection to the software subsystem would have several explicit advantages. In programs not using such contracts, major parts of the system definition effort were accomplished—especially as regards software—during the initial months of full-scale development, when the program office was engaged in staffing, learning and, in general, coming up to speed as an organization. The realities of schedule, budget, and workload often pressure the contractor to hurry the remaining tasks and unnecessarily burden the management resources of the program office. A separate system-definition contract removes this burden, forces the contractor to essentially complete system definition before the development contract is awarded, and allows more effective Air Force oversight in a crucial phase of the acquisition process.

In addition, a system definition contract can be used to acquire more complete and detailed software information—one of the lacks noted in recommendation 1—than is otherwise accessible to Air Force decision makers prior to the development phase. Besides the benefit of this information to the full-scale development competition, a system definition contract could serve as a framework for the activities of the organization described in recommendation 1 above. It would essentially force the Air

Force to come to grips with software matters during the earliest acquisition activities undertaken by contractors—exactly the activities discussed in chapter 5 as crucial to software development and as ignored by existing Air Force management practices. Thus, just as recommendation 1 aims to improve the Air Force's organizational structure, recommendation 2 aims to improve the coverage given by Air Force managers to key software development activities.

3. *Require, as contractually deliverable, the collection and mainte-nance of software project data from the Air Force and from all appropriate contractors.*

The lack of quantitative information upon which to base informed decisions is widely perceived as a major impediment to improved software management. Yet, neither prime contractors, their software subcontrac-tors, nor the program offices examined in the study made much of an effort to change this situation. One or two Air Force studies are underway (see, for example, Glore 1978) to develop a description of software relevant information that might end up as contract-deliverable information in the future. Most program offices do not collect much information on their own software management tasks, either. For the few in our study that did, the information collected was not routed to any sort of central repository in which software acquisition data could be collected and analyzed and the results made available to later programs. The one bright spot in this area is the Data and Analysis Center for Software at Griffiss Air Force Base. This effort was initiated in late 1978 to help rectify the data problem, but it is too early to evaluate its effects.

Such efforts should be continued, but the Air Force cannot afford to wait for their fruition and there is no need to do so. Whatever solution is finally adopted, it will require the expenditure of funds and the com-mitment of personnel. An immediate commitment of resources is war-ranted, and there is enough experience in today's Air Force to generate at least a partial list of data that might be required as contract deliverable. The usual argument, ''Let's wait until we know enough to collect the right data,'' is flawed in two ways. First, it implies that data collection is not cost-beneficial—an attitude unsupported by empirical evidence and nurtured by contractor's claims of high cost based on the difficulty of data collection. Second, there is no indication at present that there will ever be a complete and accurate list of of the information needed. The Air Force should generate its own list based on currently available research and on the educated judgment of experienced individuals. This list should then be negotiated as a standard contract item deliverable for future major acquisition programs. Additionally, program office guidance should require the collection of information about the conduct of Air Force software acquisition management. This effort can be guided by a similar preliminary list of the required information.

The advantages of this suggestion are several. First, the information initially generated should provide at least some benefit to Air Force decision making, especially if this recommendation is implemented together with those described above and, therefore, is engaged with the earliest relevant activities of both the contractor and the Air Force.

Second, by providing a record of statistics, decisions, and outcomes, it would begin to fill the gaps in the Air Force's ability to learn from experience. Data from the SPO might include, for example, the number, experience, and training of software personnel; the time spent on paperwork versus that spent in substantive technical analysis; the number and kinds of technical software issues first raised by SPO personnel; and the time spent and actions taken by SPO personnel in resolving those issues. Contractor data could include similar personnel information; counts of such things as number of tested instructions developed per month; actual time distributions for the various stages of development; and the like. Obviously, a useful initial list could be generated.

Third, it should furnish a better sense than is now available of the costs involved in collecting and using such data. Fourth, it should illuminate the kinds of analytic tools needed for making the best use of the available data thus providing guidance for current and future programs aimed at developing such tools. Finally, it will provide a foundation for improving the nature and quality of data collected on subsequent programs.

4.   *Identify and make better use of existing sources of software expertise.*

In cases where program directors are especially concerned with acquiring personnel skilled in software, they often rely on their own (or a friend's) personal knowledge of the whereabouts and availability of appropriate individuals. Not infrequently, attempts are made by the program director to transfer particularly skilled individuals to a program office. The fact that such efforts are both necessary and, often, successful suggests two things. First, formal personnel assignment policies and procedures are sometimes unresponsive to program office requirements. Several of those interviewed criticized the normal staffing channels. The procedures for matching available skills with open positions were seen as too random; likewise, the existing centers of expertise provided generalists where specialists were required. These problems should be better focused by further study.

The second implication is that more software talent exists than is routinely assumed to be available, but that it is hard to recognize. Some of this talent exists, for example, at the operational level in individuals who routinely apply their training and experience to a variety of Air Force mission functions. These individuals can be difficult to recognize because they may not be classified or thought of as software experts, yet their responsibilities may involve programming or systems analysis in specific—and quite relevant—mission areas. In some cases, these people have university degrees in computer science or related fields and represent an experienced—and rarely tapped—pool of software and functional area expertise. Program directors who successfully acquired needed software skills despite a shortage of formally recognized personnel often did so on the basis of personal familiarity with exceptional individuals from this pool.

Successful acquisition of embedded software may come to depend on continued and accelerated development of just this kind of pool. This does not necessarily require that the more general training and retention problems now facing the Air Force be solved; rather, one would survey the operational community, identify currently hidden resources, and develop policy mechanisms that make them available to program offices. This approach has been used informally with significant success (see program E and H, in particular), and warrants more formal attention.

External—that is, non-Air Force—consultants represent another source of software expertise that could be better utilized. Several of the program offices examined had a low opinion of the worth of consultants. Characteristically, they were called in when software problems were already evident; frequently, the only result was a detailed enumeration of those problems offered without corresponding solutions. Some suggest that this was caused by their late entry into the program and the time needed for them to become familiar with the problem at hand.

Even where consultants are part of the initial program planning, however, the results can be poor; program C (see appendix A) is a good example of mismanaged potential in this area. By contrast, program H shows the benefits available when technical-assistance contracts are well managed. There seems to be a consensus that when early and controlled use is made of external expertise, the outcome is generally improved.

With this in mind, we suggest that the Air Force develop some formal guidance as to the conditions under which acquisition program managers should consider outside expertise.

5. *Take steps to institute a formally sanctioned career path in software management.*

A full analysis of this issue is beyond the scope of the present study.

The disincentives resulting from the lack of such a career path are, however, clearly detrimental to efforts at adapting the Air Force to its growing dependence on software skills. Moreover, the issue goes beyond the present study's focus on embedded computers. Software acquisition for the full range of defense-related computer resources is involved: therefore, the incentives provided by such a career path would accrue throughout the Air Force, to say nothing of the Defense Department itself and other government departments.

A first step would be to identify the range of skills to be associated with the new career path. This is an area where more focused study is required, but one important aspect is a sensitivity to the true nature of the task. Two recent studies, Glaseman and Davis (1980) and Davis, Glaseman, and Stanley (1982) support the notion that software skills alone are not enough; expertise in system functions is also needed. What must be encouraged is a combination of skills and operational experience that leads not only to technological awareness, but also to an ability to perceive the best bridges between the technology and the mission to be served by it.

8 Extensions

This work has some relevance for concerns that go beyond the limits of the present study. Some of the more interesting potentials are briefly sketched in the following paragraphs.

How Bureaucracies Function

Viewing the Air Force as a generalized type of large bureaucratic organization, certain observations made in this study contradict current ideas in the organization adaptation literature, thereby suggesting new and potentially fruitful research directions for organizational theorists. For example, we can observe that some system program offices (for instance, those for programs E, G, and H; see appendix A) may adapt individually to environmental influences without prior adaptive measures by the larger parent organization. This suggests that environmental adaptation may proceed, for large bureaucracies, at different rates according to the level of organization in question. The current literature most often discusses bureaucratic adaptation as though it were a uniform process affecting the entire structure at one time: the bureaucracy either adapts or it does not. Moreover, if it does adapt, it does so rather slowly unless a major change occurs at the top—a frequently encountered example describes the bureaucratic upheaval that can result when a new president takes office.

By contrast, this study suggests that the bureaucratic components closest to the environment and most immediately affected by changes in it are capable of comparatively rapid adaptation. At higher levels of the organization where there is a greater distance from environmental consequences, a broader range of objectives, and new constraints on discretionary decisionmaking, adaptation may be considerably slower or absent altogether.

Furthermore, most texts describe modern bureaucracies in terms of the classic Weberian model in which, for example, standardized rules supplant individual discretion. This study suggests, however, that certain bureaucratic subunits (for instance, system program office) can and do operate largely on the basis of individual discretion and can be quite effective under certain circumstances. This is true when, for example, a program director is sensitive to the potential system-wide impact of a poorly managed software effort. In some cases where this sensitivity existed, early attention to software and innovative management techniques—implemented at the program director's discretion—led to improved acquisition experiences.

These considerations imply that a more complex and robust model of bureaucratic organizations is needed that recognizes a range of complex suborganizations with equally complex interdependencies. Within such an extended model, the notion of adaptation might then be addressed in terms of those interdependencies and in terms of such variables as environmental distance, focus of objectives, and decision-making mechanisms.

Incentives for Adaptation

An explicit contrast was drawn in this study between the adaptive capabilities of the defense contractor community and those of the Air Force. This contrast illuminates differences between public- and private-sector organizations that affect both the propensity to adapt and the speed with which adaptation occurs—at whatever level.

For example, although organizations in both sectors need to adapt, certain environmental characteristics encourage adaptation in the private sector and, by their absence, inhibit it in the public sector. These include the profit motive (without which growth in private-sector organizations would be stifled and future competitive advantage placed at risk) and the competitive market (within which there is at least some question of organizational survival). Moreover, the private sector can usually provide its personnel with incentives that many public-sector organizations, especially the military, lack—wages tied to individual performance, the possibility of rapid advancement based also on performance, and incentives to specialize in specific technical disciplines.

These differences reflect important motivating forces and some, like wage incentives, are likely to persist for the relevant future. This raises a question, not only for the Air Force, but for the Defense Department as a whole and for other departments of government: What organizational levers can be used to encourage effective adaptation to important environmental changes?

One answer suggested by these results is increased reliance on individual discretion, along with more direct and visible consequences for both good and poor results. Such consequences must invoke the incentives that are recognized by individuals who understand, for example, that wages are not a major organizational bargaining tool. Increased management responsibilities and personal and team citations for achievement are examples of these kinds of incentives. In turn, their use implies a more complex notion of the standard operating procedures than is currently applied in large bureaucracies. Thus, we would suggest research into the bureaucratic incentive structure and the circumstances that call for a suspension of mandatory standards in favor of discretionary action. These ideas also support the need, mentioned ealier, for a more representative model of bureaucratic organizations—one that places appropriate emphasis on discretionary decision making.

Organizing for the Future

The results of this study might also be extended, in an anticipatory way, to the emerging influence of recent advances in electronic-circuit integration. With the development and rapid evolution of very highly integrated circuits, devices now exist that defy categorization as either hardware or software. Functionally, these devices embody characteristics from each; not surprisingly, therefore, they are referred to as "firmware" devices (see *Aviation Week and Space Technology* 1981).

Many of those interviewed voiced apprehension that the Department of Defense will relive its current software problems during the rapidly approaching firmware era. The consequences of mismatches between management practices and managed processes in the software-acquisition environment should alert policymakers to the need for anticipatory responses to the firmware acquisition environment. It should also motivate them to bring thought, experience, and experiment to bear on a problem of surpassing importance: Are there optimum structures for organizations acquiring and supporting defense systems—systems composed of an ever-more-complex meld of hardware, software, and firmware?

Appendix A:
Software Acquisition
Management Case
Studies

System A

Narrative Overview

The original program started in 1968, and the designated prime contractor was given overall system integration responsibilities. Two years later, in 1970, the program's classification was changed from "development" to "modification"; in 1974, the Air Force took over systems integration responsibility from the prime contractor. (Apparently, there were not enough funds to pay the contractor to do system integration.)

There are important differences between a modification program and a development program. In the case of a modification program, primary responsibility is with Air Force Logistics Command rather than with Systems Command. The former group has few of the developmental resources required for major system acquisition programs. Yet, many modification programs are, like system A, primarily developmental in nature. Thus, the lack of organizational resources and of a development mind-set has been viewed as a main contributor to the problems experienced by system A.

The estimates of storage requirements for mission software started at 8000 words (8K) and increased over the years to 16K, 32K, and 65K words. Current plans call for the addition of 256K of auxiliary memory by 1983. The mission software is designed for ease of modification, a requirement in the initial system specifications. Software development was undertaken with little discipline and no explicit plans for configuration management. The Air Force paid minimum attention to software management during the early part of this program; one result was inadequate consideration of software testing. Certain needed test facilities were never provided to the program; the system itself acted as a software laboratory.

Except for the program director—of which there have been thirteen in the twelve years the program has been active—software personnel were assigned to the program from the engineering group in the Aeronautical Systems Division.

Several contractors are working on system A; the job of the program office is to integrate their efforts to produce a working system. Some

83

external help was made available to the SPO when an engineer who wrote much of the original mission software went to work for a company that allowed him to work as a consultant to the Air Force Program Office.

System A's mission software design was frozen in July 1978—ten years after the start of the program. This delay was due partly to changes in the system's mission that forced a major revision of the mission software. When the revision decision was made, an audit was conducted that compared the "as designed" software specifications with the "as produced" specifications. It was discovered that the two did not match well; the design specifications had not been kept up to date and did not agree with the later baselined version. In other words, system behavior could not be traced to the original requirements.

The subsequent changes were not received from the user until September 1978, and were to be implemented by the following June. However, it became clear that the contractor could not meet this schedule and, in April 1979, the program office generated its own update that implemented the major changes. During this same period, ongoing operational tests were producing additional small, poorly documented changes to the mission software. As a result, the contractor's own efforts to keep up with software changes and to generate useful documentation were seriously hampered.

As in most programs, a computer resources working group was formed; however, for system A, this occurred during the test and evaluation stage, ten years after the start of the program. The lack of early attention to software testing and support planning has contributed to the frequently heard assessment of this program as a software disaster.

Frequent informal coordinating meetings took the place of formal reviews at first. At present, program office oversight is achieved through the following:

1. The consultant contract mentioned earlier.
2. The late-formed, but now reasonably effective, working group.
3. The relevant Air Logistics Center.

Problem Summary

Software costs and schedule were grossly underestimated. The contractor failed to appreciate the importance of software to the system's mission. Both the Air Force and the contractor had unrealistic views of the ease with which software could be changed. The contractor, moreover, did not really expect major software changes and resisted them when they were requested. Other problems stemmed from management decisions that permitted computer hardware suppliers to write specifications for software subcontractors.

System B

Narrative Overview

The Air Force (helped by potential contractors) produced a request for proposal (RFP) that set forth some preliminary system-level performance specifications. The winning contractor responded to the RFP with expanded specifications containing (1) software requirements in narrative format and (2) a set of top-level flow charts, including descriptions of algorithms, formats, and data structures. The contractor was to decide how and where processing was to be accomplished and took complete charge of the competition for subcontracted software.

The full-scale development contract for system B was awarded in January 1970. The first operational test occurred in early 1972; the first production model was delivered in September 1974. Approximately 300 systems are now in existence out of an anticipated total of over 700, (not counting foreign military sales).

System B's contract, like that of system A, preceded the implementation of Air Force Regulation 800-14. Consequently, no formal software specifications were required, and software acquisition was guided primarily by existing technical order documentation standards. Under these standards, computer programs were delivered to the field and controlled as supplemental system information, not as major system components.

The program office gave no special attention to software. The contractor specified the initial requirements and was then expected to deliver an appropriate software package. The program office made no attempt to monitor how the software was produced, and though the contractor did submit monthly progress reports on individual software components, there were no formal reviews devoted exclusively to software.

The Air Force's primary software management roles seemed to be monitoring overall system development and approving documentation. In rare situations, technical details were addressed—for example, one algorithm was changed from that originally proposed by the contractor to one suggested by the Air Force as more appropriate. However, the contractor is rarely required to take customer advice in such matters. As was the case with system E, system B SPO personnel reported frequent interaction between themselves and the contractor in addition to the required formal reviews.

Problem Summary

The software design was not baselined early enough; this generated serious problems with subsequent efforts to develop software for automated test equipment. Some of the engine diagnostic software development—part of the system's built-in test equipment (BITE)—was originally assigned to a hardware group that did not understand the task; this, in addition to unspecified problems with the software for a major mission subsystem, contributed additional cost growth and schedule delays.

System C

Narrative Overview

System C was originally part of a larger program that used off-the-shelf computational resources. The system was intended only as an initial prototype; off-the-shelf hardware and support software was used because of its apparent cost-effectiveness. (No one listened to early warnings that this could be illusory.)

In March 1972, an RFP was released; in December 1972, the hardware and support software prime contract was awarded. This contract involved two major subcontracts: a mission computer from one supplier and, from another, the operating system, support software, and a front-end computer. In mid-1973, a mission software prime contractor was chosen. The hardware and support software contractor was to provide inputs for later use by the mission software contractor. These split contracts were agreed to by the program office and by the operational user; the arrangement was initially proposed to ease the Air Force's management task.

The initial hardware was to be installed in July 1973. Some of the prototype hardware was identical to that ultimately deliverable; other equipment was built up from commercial equivalents. The Air Force intended to use this makeshift hardware environment to develop both the support and the mission software.

Because very little software and hardware expertise was available in the program office, a "watchdog" contractor was engaged to coordinate all of the tasks associated with computer resources. This contractor concurred in the original decision to acquire off the shelf and suggested appropriate vendors. By September 1973, the mission software contractor had been given a three-volume system specification written by the watchdog contractor. Volume 1 was an overview of the entire procurement program, volume 2 listed hardware and high-level support software requirements, and volume 3, the operational (mission) software requirements.

Both software contractors had problems developing their specifications. For one thing, the Air Force had trouble defining exactly what was wanted (the user's requirements were largely unknown). Moreover, the watchdog contractor was somewhat naive regarding the particular mission involved; their charter as systems engineer and authorship of the initial system specifications locked them into an inflexible advocacy posture. In retrospect, the program office was also relatively shortsighted and, as mentioned above, poorly cognizant of its own needs. As a result, rigidity was substituted for competence and innovative thinking. Strict adherence to the original specification was demanded even after it became clear that major problems were developing. This led to overmanagement and a failure to let the contractors' comparative advantages work for them. For example, the relationship between the program office and the contractors was constrained too much by regulations that cut heavily into the time available for monitoring development. The program office ultimately rejected the first software specification; if they had paid more attention to software initially, they might have avoided the schedule slip caused by the need to redo the specification. Similarly, the hardware specification, although deliverable six months after contract award, was actually available only after sixteen.

The support software subcontractor seemed unable to construct a reliable operating system. With no benchmark requirements for the software, the government had no baseline for solving this problem. Coupled with uneven prototype hardware, this led to huge problems in troubleshooting. The troubleshooting problem, in turn, was compounded by the lack of useful diagnostic software for either the operating system, the data management system, or the mission software.

Both preliminary and critical design reviews were passed primarily because of the politics that forced the program to continue. To the user, however, these reviews were failures as far as demonstrated functional potential was concerned. Unfortunately, these opinions had limited influence because the user's technical people did not communicate well with their own management or with program office personnel.

Another problem was the failure of the software engineering task. Neither prime contractor had an established capability in software engineering. Although the mission software contractor had a reputation as a software house, they had never been involved in a project as large and complex as this one. Neither contractor recognized the relationship between engineering and software development. The program office, in its turn, did not call the contractors to task quickly enough because their failures were not apparent until the mission software contractor tried to use the support software. The Air Force was also reluctant to pursue a tough stand with respect to cost growth. By the time system C was cancelled, the original computer hardware cost estimate had grown from $10.3 million to $45 million (more than fourfold), and the initial software estimate (total for mission and support software) had grown from $1.3 million to approximately $20 million (almost twentyfold).

At first, work on the mission software specification appeared to move smoothly. Special teams produced computer program configuration item (CPCI) specifications in the areas of communication processing, database systems, the exercise data generator, and the display computers. The next step was to design the individual computer programs associated with each CPCI.

Coding started using the ''as designed'' specifications, but these did not contain sufficient detail to guarantee effective development—there were no system-level flowcharts, let alone charts for individual programs. Moreover, neither algorithms nor input/output requirements were well identified. None of the detail one would expect to find on a procurement of system C's complexity was available. Furthermore, since there was no coordination among individual programming groups, there were severe problems integrating various pieces of code into program modules. The results were (1) the integrated modules fell apart; (2) the code was impossible to troubleshoot; (3) no requirements baseline existed against which to compare functional performance; (4) documentation was inadequate; and (5) the subcontractor's engineering efforts were poorly managed.

As these troubles evolved, storage requirements grew from an initial 96K words to 160K words. However, even with 160K, the original performance requirements could not be met. By May 1974, it was clear that the support software subcontractor could not produce an adequate operating system. At this point, the government gave the task to the mission software contractor and gave them an additional $2.7 million (taken from the hardware prime). This contractor then renewed relationships with the original two software subcontractors.

By this time, two independent Air Force review groups had been formed, each headed by a general officer. These groups accused the program of overmanagement, weak enforcement of Air Force policies, and poor documentation.

Another group, the system investigative team, was formed to referee confrontations between the watchdog contractor and the two prime contractors. This group was formed because of a perceived lack of feedback during the developmental process and a failure to assign systems integration responsibility for system C. This group eventually became the default system integrator.

Other problems included personnel turnover and inadequate training of program office personnel in the relevant technical disciplines. Our respondents noted that the people working on technical problems frequently did not understand their roles in the context of the larger system. Thus, some of their decisions, while appropriate in the narrow sense, were ill-considered for the overall program. One example mentioned earlier was that no diagnostic software was produced to aid development and support efforts.

Ultimately, lack of results led to selective funding cuts. This compressed schedules, and it became clear (in 1975) that the program was in danger of cancellation.

By 1977, the Air Force had trimmed the system's operational requirements and revamped the management plan. The new approach was to base future production decisions on the performance of available facilities. This meant, however, that untested hardware would be used to prove untested software.

In mid-1977, the system still was not ready for a field test; many unresolved hardware and software problems remained. The software needed constant support; it contained many implementation errors and was badly documented. Moreover, troubleshooting was almost impossible without considerable handholding by the original developer, and the lack of diagnostic capability made matters considerably worse.

Originally, hardware diagnostics were to be produced at the subsystem level. However, this was impossible because not even system-level diagnostic requirements had been specified. As a result, the evolving mission software was used as a system diagnostic tool. The mission software contractor was not required to produce diagnostic software either, even though they were on contract for system-level testing. This implies either that they would not take the initiative, or that the Air Force could not define requirements well enough, or both. (The contract, it should be noted, was of the cost-plus-incentive fee type; the incentive, therefore, was to maximize profits, not to spend them on developing new or modified software.)

In addition to these problems, the program had relatively austere funding for logistics support. Because of the problems so far discussed, spares were used fairly steadily from early in the project to support the test version of the system. Thus, many support resources were used up during the development phase.

On 15 June 1978, the mission software contractor was fired as manager of the overall software development effort. They were still on contract to produce the mission software, but an Air Force user group assumed management responsibility. This group assigned tasks, dealt with problems, and reviewed the contractor's subsequent performance.

As a part of this initiative, the program office was required to concur on all of the user's directives to the contractor. That contractor ultimately used fewer people and produced better software more efficiently. The prime mover of this Air Force management effort was the deputy program director, a civilian who had been on the program since the first days, knew it well, and was a strong manager. He had responsibility for the whole organizational tree, with the power to reallocate people and other resources at both Air Force and contractor levels (although at the contractor level all he could do was make strong recommendations).

Between June 1978 and March 1979, many software problems were found and fixed. This effort was coordinated by a production-configuration working group that included members from the relevant contractors, the participating users, and the program office. Some problems requiring major redesign were documented and left for the production phase. The March 1979 system tests revealed a reduced-capability system at least partially useful to some users and surprisingly well within most response-time specifications. On the other hand, the criteria for evaluation had also been trimmed to reflect a more prudent view of system C's operational responsibilities.

Today, the Air Force is devoting resources to an alternative program that is also expected to use equipment and software acquired off the shelf and integrated in a later phase. The new system is a scaled-down version of the original system C program incorporating many of the lessons learned. One important difference is that the user, not a contractor, will develop the software for the new system. Many believe that an off-the-shelf effort could now be effective, given the last ten years of progress in the relevant technologies; however, this is not a certainty. There has also been some learning in the relevant mission area since 1971 as well as in the management of complex programs. However, the user's requirements for reliability, maintainability, and so on still impose severe constraints on the applicability of the latest technology.

Problem Summary

There never was a formal requirements allocation process for system C's software. The initial system specification was written by committee and included system design information as well as functional specifications. Inclusion by the vendor of a software design generated by the Air Force allowed for both easy contract acceptance and easy assignment of blame (to the Air Force) in case of trouble. The program office thought in terms of one target machine while the user had several options in mind. In the final analysis, there was never a useful software development machine;

the Air Force had to use the mission computers themselves to develop and test both mission and support software.

The initial specification of off-the-shelf hardware and support software was perhaps the crucial error. There were no preliminary or critical design reviews for the support software because off-the-shelf procurements had no Air Force standard review/audit requirements; thus, fundamental problems were not caught. The contractors should have run an integrated hardware and support software development program, but the Air Force gave them neither time nor money to do so. As a result, neither contractor enthusiastically embraced either the software engineering or system integration tasks.

System D

Narrative Overview

System D was originally funded by the intelligence community. The system as initially described had excess processing capacity and another user wanted to add several tasks to its repertoire. The result was an agreement to service the second user when processing resources remaining from the major mission could be allocated to secondary tasks. As a result of this agreement, an engineering change proposal (ECP) was requested six months into the full-scale development phase of system D. The contractor was given a deadline of two weeks to answer this ECP, and their response specified a $1.4 million modification to the original contract. We were told that the Air Force neither saw, requested to see, nor evaluated the technical analyses behind the response.

The engineering change essentially dominated the software development effort—95 percent of the conversation in meetings was about the added mission software and the impact it was likely to have on overall system acquisition. However, the full scope of the change emerged only gradually as the interfaces between the new system and the other necessary facilities clarified. Contingency funds to respond to some of the problems came from management reserve, but even though the change was large enough to warrant a $1.4 million extension in the program budget, there was no corresponding extension in the program schedule.

Certain earlier decision set the stage for the resulting situation, soon blamed almost entirely on this ECP. For example, two months after contract award the SPO decided to delay formal software configuration management until the end of the development phase. (This was intended to give the software contractor maximum flexibility.) Another decision, made prior to contract award, was to specify one computer for all of system D's computational requirements—a decision that was not rereviewed when the ECP was requested.

The single-computer concept led to immediate problems. The computer was installed and found to be just adequate for the tasks originally specified. Meeting the ECP requirements with a single computer was out of the question.

The Air Force also failed to define contractual milestones for software or hardware development until late in the program, when problems were obvious. Nor were there contingency plans, in case such problems did occur. Consequently, the prime contractor's review of, and recovery from, a major software design problem led to a one-year schedule delay.

The Air Force accused the contractors of poor systems engineering and inadequate management of software development. From then on, the software subcontractor was required to report on milestones defined by the Air Force. Twenty-four months into a thirty-three-month schedule, the software subcontractor assigned an in-house troubleshooter. Teams from the user's organization recommended demonstrations of the capabilities being produced. Even though the contractor eventually passed all of the reviews and system tests, there are still important system ECP items outstanding. The system is now operational and, in spite of continuing acquisition-related problems, is seen by the user as a success story.

Problem Summary

Certain initial decisions regarding the adequacy of computer hardware were not reviewed before the SPO approved a major modification to system specifications. This resulted in cost growth and schedule delays as the necessary revisions were made on an emergency basis. Poor contract management (such as lack of formal milestones, delayed configuration control) contributed to a one-year schedule slip, as did failure to perceive an overly ambitious software subsystem design. Documentation was ineffective, as were more informal efforts at user-SPO-contractor communications. Overall, an inadequate job of software engineering.

System E

Narrative Overview

The only documentation initially required for system E was the system specification. Thus, although the system program office received rough versions of software specifications as these documents evolved, the contractor was allowed considerable flexibility in meeting documentation format requirements. This made it difficult for the Air Force to develop a test program because less information was available. On the other hand, this approach also decreased the vast amount of paperwork usually associated with engineering change proposals and other documentation, freeing resources for more active monitoring of technical details. Therefore, although the Air Force had little of its customary control over the contents of the software specifications, their overall right of system approval kept pressure on the contractor both to perform and to keep the Air Force involved throughout.

This experiment in interpreting documentation policy allowed top-level control of requirements specifications, but did not require formal written reviews of them. Software document approval was moved to the end of the full-scale development period. This experiment also permitted more technical interaction between program-office personnel and the contractor's engineers between formal reviews. In short, there was more contact than usual between the Air Force and the contractor.

Internal software meetings occurred weekly at the contractor's installation, and results (including any problems raised) were regularly reported back to the program office. The formal review structure was further augmented by feedback from tests and from independent verification and validation (V & V) programs carried out by the Wright Avionics Laboratory and the relevant Air Logistics Centers. Reviews were effectively continuous.

The program office participated in early decisions involving, for instance, the chief programmer concept, the use of a high-order language, and documentation requirements for the computer program development plan. As the program moved through full-scale development, the Air Force used two oversight groups. One group monitored the contractor's technical performance, but played only a limited role in managing the overall development program. The other group managed the overall acquisition process and dealt only indirectly with the technical aspects of the program. Thus, the focus of system E's preliminary and critical design reviews on management issues was acceptable because technical problems were being resolved informally. The latter forum is absent in more conventional programs, and it may be that the customary focus of formal reviews acts to obscure technical problems. The management structure used on system E could have led to earlier identification of technical problems than might otherwise have been the case.

Overall, software development for system E was very successful. However, there were some problems—subsystem X is a good example. The Air Force saw subsystem X as a digital device, but this was not reflected in the contract. As a result, the contractor initially assigned responsibility for this device to the wrong group, which produced a totally unsatisfactory set of requirements. Not until program office managers learned of the problem was the assignment corrected and a satisfactory set of specifications developed.

Another technical problem influenced by the program office was an interface timing problem caused by an overspecified requirement. This stated that the latest available data should be used in each of a number of cyclic computations, making it necessary to move data during the computations. Since data from the previous cycle was always available and was adequate for the computations involved, the program office encouraged the contractor to use that data instead, eliminating the need for data movement during the computation cycle, thereby reducing processing complexity.

The essential point of both problems is that Air Force management was directly involved in solutions at both the technical and managerial levels—contrary to the usual experience of most program offices.

Because of the lack of complete and detailed specifications, a certain amount of money is being spent on changes that might not have been necessary if conventional techniques had been used. Overall, however, the changes required are probably fewer and better considered than they would have been otherwise.

The program director also knew that individually processed software changes could nickel and dime the program to death. Therefore, he negotiated a software contract in which changes were to be grouped into blocks, the specifics of each block to be determined over the acquisition period. Theoretically, only those changes that survive an evaluation effort are implemented under such a contract. After evaluation, they are assigned priorities and applied in one large, controlled group.

System procurement was lead initially by an enthusiastic and hardworking colonel who was director of a pre-program office organization. As an operationally experienced officer, he was dedicated to implementing a cost-effective software effort. Another influential factor was the configuration steering group (CSG) formed in late 1974, which included high-level participants from the Air Staff and from the user community. The primary function of the steering group was determining cost and performance trade-offs, selecting effective alternatives, and establishing guidelines. The basic policy guiding these efforts was that the contractor design to fit the cost estimate.

Since software was not a major consideration during source selection, the pre-program office was not staffed in this area. When the request for proposal (RFP) for full-scale development was being contemplated, however, software emerged as a significant component.

A government civilian was assigned responsibility for the software content of the RFP. This person had a technical background but little experience in computers or software. At the time the RFP was written, most of the decisions regarding the functions and performance of the system had already been made by the steering group. Air Force Regulation 800–14 had not yet been approved, but draft copies had been widely circulated and everyone knew that compliance would be required. To meet this requirement, a software expert was hired. This was the first entry of software expertise into the system E acquisition picture. As it turned out, however, less then one page in the RFP dealt explicitly with system software. This material spelled out the following:

1. The requirement for use of a high-order programming language.
2. The requirement for a communications bus architecture.
3. The mission computer software architecture.
4. The intent to comply with Air Force Regulation 800–14.
5. The requirement for built-in test capability.

The system specification did contain detailed requirements for the functional capabilities of computational subsystems, and several major pieces of mission software were identified in the contract as computer program configuration items. Air Force Regulation 800–14 also required that specific management attention be given to these items in the form of formal reviews and documentation.

After the contract was awarded, a program office software expert was sent to the prime contractor to learn how computer programs were developed. He became part of their software engineering team (as opposed to participating in management) and had a large positive influence on the Air Force's management efforts.

Another group that influenced the program was a cost effectiveness working group with members from Air Force Systems Command, Air Force Logistics Command, and the user community. Only a few details are known of the extent and direction of this group's influence on the program. It is known that the group made two important recommendations:

1. That a software focal point be established in the program office to help resolve software problems throughout the program.
2. That an independent effort be mounted to validate and verify the developed software.

Some acquisition logistics personnel believe that reviews by outside personnel (such as consultants) are a waste of time. Since such reviews are usually instituted toward the end of a program, they characteristically operate under severe time constraints. The reviewers usually do not have enough time to understand the system, let alone identify and solve significant problems. There is evidence that such reviews did not usually identify new problems, and that those identified were not often accompanied by useful remedies. In this case, however, external consultants contributed importantly by identifying an individual with the expertise needed for starting the recommended focal point. This person, who was appointed as Assistant Chief Engineer/Software Manager about six months after the contract was awarded, formed a computer resources working group chartered to do the things required by Air Force Regulation 800-14. A principal part of their effort was preparing and refining the computer resources integrated support plan (CRISP), as required by that regulation.

During the ensuing year, anywhere from five to thirty people were involved at various times in the preparation of the plan. This group influenced software design, made technical trade-off decisions, and designated test procedures for the mission and support software. The software focal point also coordinated the formation of a number of additional ad hoc groups aimed at several specific issues. For example, a software action team was charged with coordinating the work of the various software actors in the program office.

Problem Summary

Beyond a general feeling that Air Force participation could be more technically focused, the system E program office faced only moderate software management problems.

System F

Narrative Overview

The original request for proposal for this system was released late in 1975, and a full-scale development contract was awarded the following January. As with most other programs in this study, there was no separate system definition contract for system F. (Our respondent felt that many such contracts are largely political in nature.)

System F was supplied with only poorly defined requirements from the system users and from certain regulatory agencies. For example, since system F will have a nuclear capability, certain Nuclear Regulatory Commission regulations were applicable. It was not immediately clear, however, what impact they would have on system requirements.

System F uses a distributed computer architecture. Two computers perform the fundamental control and mission functions; each provides backup for certain critical tasks of the other. A number of additional computers are associated with critical subsystems, and all these computational resources are interconnected by a standard communications bus. The computational system was designed with spare storage in mind, but storage resources for both mission computers were filled early in the development period. The original storage planned for each was 32,000 (32K) words. One now has 64K (and is full), the other remains at 32K (and is also full). Even so, the potential for adding 32K words of extra storage to these machines is considered as meeting the officially imposed requirement for spare capacity.

According to program office personnel, the RFP for system F was produced using informal groups of technical experts, each group corresponding to a particular subsystem associated with the overall product. For example, a software group produced the draft software specification. What they produced however, was a very general list of system-level performance specifications; software requirements were addressed only indirectly.

The government's approach to managing system F's acquisition is based on a ''hands-off'' management philosophy. All that the contractor need do is deliver a ''clean tape'' at a predetermined date.

The SPO's software manager feels that as systems become more and more integrated, the hardware/software interfaces become less clearly definable. He feels it is folly to maintain that a hardware/software trade-off can be made with any degree of accuracy at the time a system specification is done. Moreover, because of the blurring boundary between hardware and software, hardware errors are very hard to distinguish from software errors; thus the customer's best decision is simply to require, as was done on system F, delivery of an error-free program tape. This requirement is seen by some as one key to more successful acquisition of mission software. In fact, built into system F's contract is a six-month grace period following delivery during which testing is carried out and discrepancies can be resolved at no cost to the customer.

System F's managers do not agree (as stated by contractor personnel) that flight programs rarely fail. For example, they pointed out that the last ''clean'' tape they received (for an earlier system) had contained well over 100 errors, of which nearly one third were safety related. Such problems result, in some cases, from external influences such as the imposition of preselected standard computational resources. System F's mission computer was imposed in this fashion as government furnished equipment, as was the use of a high-order programming language. These decisions can lead to problems when contractors are unfamiliar with the mandated equipment, especially when related software must be developed rapidly. For example, system F uses the contractor's version of a standard communications bus. The original bus-interface software did not work properly because the subcontractor did not adhere to specifications. These problems vanished the second time around, but not before program schedule and costs had been affected. In order to deal with similar problems that might arise further into system development, the Air Force inserted specific new clauses in the contract to help the prime contractor manage his major subcontractors.

The operational user's visibility into this program is maintained by a team of software specialists that monitor the contractor's progress via technical coordination meetings. While being so monitored, the storage requirement for one subsystem grew from 160K to 250K words. The explanations given were that (1) this was the first time such high accuracy had been required in this type of system; (2) gaining such accuracy is a complex technical challenge requiring correspondingly complex software; and (3) the initial estimate of 160K words was only a guess, based on insufficient knowledge and experience about the real size of the job involved.

At this writing (late 1980), the preliminary and critical software design reviews have been passed, and the design of system F has been frozen. The reviews identified no significant software problems; indeed, software reliability is the firmest contract requirement and is backed up by penalties and incentives in certain areas. Nevertheless, software development is approximately six months behind schedule.

Most of system F's documentation will be deliverable in 1982 or 1983, when the system is delivered. The SPO expects to enhanced its accuracy by delaying its delivery in this way (as in system E). Meanwhile, reports from the technical coordination meetings provide one source of informal documentation and act as a useful communication device.

Site X will eventually take over support for mission software, and is currently testing several of the more independent modules. There are other test facilities, including a complex simulator facility at the contractor's installation that maintains a great deal of supporting hardware and software. A major benefit of these facilities is that the software and hardware in the simulator can be made identical to that in the operational system, thus enabling tests of significant validity.

Problem Summary

Our respondents felt that the biggest problems with embedded software were externally imposed cost and schedule variations. There were some technical problems, but nothing generally catastrophic; however, cost and schedule pressures can obscure problems that become visible only later in the cycle, when they are more expensive to fix. It is interesting to note that even the management resource is diluted. The software manager on system F has been tapped by Congress to manage (concurrently) an improvement program for system E.

System G

Narrative Overview

The system program office began working on the requirements for system G by forming a steering group consisting of operational users, air staff personnel, and other Department of Defense participants. The first requirements document estimated the system costs at $100 million, but private expectations were closer to $60 million. A middle-management working group was formed to reduce estimated costs and formalize the requirements. This group coordinated their efforts with steering group personnel and hired an independent contractor to generate a refined set of software requirements. However, after three months, little progress had been made. The specification produced by this group was not sophisticated enough (in a managerial sense) to form the basis for contract negotiations.

A software expert hired by the program office eventually perceived that no one, including the independent contractor, had bothered to understand the user's requirements. This individual undertook to understand them and began to rewrite the specifications himself. In time, he became the informal communications channel for all software questions and changes. Basically, he accomplished two things: he edited the specifications into mission-oriented language that the users could better understand, and he formalized the requirements documents while at the same time coordinating them with users' concerns about changes to the system. Eventually, other Air Force technicians worked to refine the evolving requirements documents while the expert shifted his attention to managing communication between the users and the members of the steering committee.

These efforts amounted to an informal, but highly effective, requirements validation study. The specifications as originally written were fed back to users in their own language, calling their attention to potential problems. Much was learned during this stage. Frequently, users had not really understood what their specifications said and were enthusiastic about the opportunity to rectify things before development began. During the two months it took to do this, an excellent rapport was developed between the program office and the user community. This generated trust in program office efforts to cut costs and in its ability to respond accurately to user needs.

These efforts led eventually to a decision to request bids on a formal system definition contract to do the following:

1. To buy time to better understand the requirements *before* software development was attempted.
2. To buy more information about a particularly crucial piece of equipment.

Three such contracts were awarded at $1 million each, for a total of $3 million. Each contractor recieved a draft RFP. It required him to (1) identify and estimate computer resource costs; (2) do a requirements analysis and preliminary system design (which reduced risk by requiring software development specifications, trade studies on software development methodology, a computer program development study, and so on; (3) provide a list of validated requirements, with information on which ones could be eased if necessary and how much money would be saved in each case; and (4) identify the major cost items in the specification, suggesting how system G might be acquired less expensively.

The contractors were hesitant at first about revealing their design strategies; for them to do so was to risk losing their competitive edge. This problem was overcome when the Air Force guaranteed to hold individual designs secret from other participants. By mid-contract, each contractor had suggested changes based on their own perceptions of important cost items. Informal meetings of program-office, user, and consultant personnel generated a document that, by combining those changes, identified about $15 million in potential savings. This document was reviewed with operational users, then presented to the steering group.

At first the users would not accept the major cost-reducing changes. The program office then developed $10 million worth of ''negative options'' such as leasing instead of buying spares, computers, and so on. These were inserted into the development contract, the idea being to invoke the less expensive options if necessary to cut costs. This approach was subsequently rejected and that of ''positive options'' substituted. Under this new arrangement, the Air Force could purchase certain options later, if funding was available. The primary impact of all this was a slip in the development schedule. Moreover, the program office had to include the so-called positive options during source selection anyway, since it was clear from the system definition study that the program would require most of them.

On the other hand, the system definition phase resulted in three very good technical proposals. The system is currently in development and still relies on the informal technical oversight mechanism initiated by the program-office software expert. (He is currently the system engineer on another program.) The definition contract also resulted in a two-month head start on the acquisition process.

Today there are still low-level requirements problems, but the excellent rapport between the program office and operational users is expected to help resolve them. The system passed its software design reviews three months into the contract. The $3 million system definition contract therefore bought the following:

A $10 to $15 million cost reduction.

Approximately $500,000 of progress on acquisition tasks.

Problem Summary.

At this writing, it is too early to evaluate system G's software effort. Thus far, however, the program office has had a very good handle on most of the key variables that have influenced the outcome of other software projects: technical expertise, user coordination, and good information.

System H

Narrative Overview

The program office was formed in September 1977 to continue part of a larger program that originated in June 1975. After the larger program was cancelled, considerable attention was focused on ways to improve the aspect of the original mission that was served by system H.

A system definition contract was granted to the current prime contractor in October 1977. This contract was funded at $8 to $10 million and was to produce a detailed study of the modifications needed to satisfy the new requirements of the system. During this effort, the computational subsystem was examined in terms of the size of the hardware and the functions allotted to software. The key question here was, "How much software from the canceled program could be used in the new one?"

The system definition contract generated a computer program development plan, recommendations for software support facilities, and an assessment of alternative program languages. The program also inherited certain management and technical resources from its cancelled predecessor. System H was given an initial operational capability (IOC) date of December 1982.

Software requirements for the program came from two main sources. First, novel algorithms developed and coded for the earlier system had to be converted and tailored to the system H environment. Second, control and display changes were required. Users were consulted on the features they would find most effective, and their ideas were solicited on how to implement the changes. The fortunate result is that early informal discussions at the system level resulted in explicitly considered—rather than de facto—software decisions.

Initially, the program office did not have much software expertise; most of the staff were hardware engineers. However, twenty to twenty-five software analysts borrowed from the contractor did much of the software work for the program office. Many of these individuals were carried over from the earlier program; in fact, most of the initial software managment team was trained on it. As one result, the computer subsystem was specified much as it was for the original system, and a watchdog contractor was employed to oversee software activities.

The watchdog will conduct verification and validation exercises as the software evolves. Currently, they hold informal technical reviews with all of the subsystem managers every few weeks, receive briefings about ongoing work, and observe existing and emerging problems. They also publish monthly reports on what is learned, advising the Air Force on the existence and potential impact of coordination problems and recommending approaches for their solution. The value of such regular, integrated, in-depth monitoring of a complex program is hard to overestimate.

The watchdog contractor also attends formal and informal program reviews and meetings of the several specialized groups working on the program. They provide technical visibility to the program office, but they do not have access to the budgetary aspects of the program. They are expected to identify risky design decisions and have developed some software analysis tools to aid this effort. They were involved with system H in the requirements-conceptualization phase and participated in many of the initial decisions regarding requirements and implementation decisions. Thus they have the big picture, can identify important targets of opportunity, and can make recommendations to both management and technical personnel. They also maintain one person on location at the prime contractor where the mission software is being developed.

The Air Force required software documentation milestones that would be responsive to Military Standards, but that would not exactly match the official format. However, this applied only to mission software; for support software, the standards were followed exactly. Some structure is also imposed by a configuration management plan developed and approved early in full-scale development.

In November 1978, the software passed a preliminary design review implemented using separate panels drawn from the Air Force, the prime contractor, and the watchdog contractor. Other participants came from Air Force Logistics Command, the relevant Air Logistics Centers, and the using command.

The design review was preceded by two weeks of documentation reviews and question preparation to ensure a successful and technically relevant meeting. The Air Force addressed inquiries to the contractor where risky or questionable elements were found in the development plan, and they wrote discrepancy reports on software requirements to guide discussions. In other words, there was a clear-cut plan for an effective review.

Part of the plan included a two-week visit to the contractor's plant. Three days were devoted exclusively to software and, in particular, to the requirements of the mission software. During this period, additional inquiries and discrepancy reports were written from briefings given during the design review. The contractor was required to respond immediately to these issues. Meetings about software were staggered to allow Air Force software personnel to attend them all. The configuration group placed inquiries and discrepancy reports in their order of priority and scheduled the future resolution of issues not immediately resolved.

Meetings with contractors were cut off in midafternoon every day during the review period, and an Air Force staff meeting was held to go over responses to the discrepancy documents in private. These were placed in categories, rereviewed, and used in writing Air Force position documents for presentation to the contractor's chief engineer.

The critical design review procedure was modified slightly as a result of experiences with the preliminary review. A two-week document review was carried out by user and logistics command personnel, but meetings at the contractor's organization were limited to one week to minimize disruption at the plant. Software problems were dealt with by the same people who were involved with them at the earlier review. Immediately thereafter, the software reviewers prepared and distributed memos on the problems they saw and on the Air Force positions taken regarding them.

The computer resources working group for this program was restricted to looking at the support area because (1) there was not enough time to include all areas under the auspices of the group and (2) it was apparently important to the program office that software not be seen as requiring unique treatment. Working group membership includes the Air Logistics Center responsible for mission software, another Air Logistics Center, Air Force Acquisition Logistics Division, the user, and the testing community.

A controls and displays working group meets as needed to monitor the status of software in that area. In addition, there is an operational-test working group made up of personnel from the contractor, testing, and support communities.

Originally, system H was on a relatively easy schedule, but pressures have increased because of the cancellation of the parent program, the subsequent decision to add capability to system H, and the establishment of a firm forty-month operational date. Another source of pressure came from a major change in requirements to allow the removal of a number of redundant operational tapes in favor of relocating one centrally. This led to many additional changes and pushed the program into a situation where software design, development, and testing were going on in parallel.

Problem Summary

The program office perceives its number one problem as a lack of funding to do things properly. First to be cut when funding was decreased were certain system reliability requirements; second were hardware requirements in the area of qualification testing; third, integration requirements, and so on. Moreover, the first year of system H's development contract was funded at a very low level relative to other program outlays. Further budget cuts are now under consideration, so the program office is looking for additional ways to cut costs. Software configuration management might be one area affected; and certain documentation may not be produced. Clearly, program offices can have little control over budgets, manpower resources, and program priorities.

Appendix B:
Software Development
Contractor Case
Studies

Contractor ABF

ABF's overall approach to software development is guided by the development of their proposal, which is evolved through the production of integration block diagrams (described below) and continues into software development specifications and, eventually, into software product specifications.

ABF maintains an advanced design group that assesses the cost of prospective new programs in terms of the size and complexity of the required development effort. This group also blocks out the type of program that ABF might mount in response to a request for proposal (RFP). The group's products are preliminary cost, schedule, size, and weight specifications, together with a plan for expanding these estimates in more detail should corporate management decide to pursue the contract. At ABF, forty percent of this group have advanced degrees. Most are Electronics Engineers, but about five percent have computer-science degrees. There are few programmers; instead, ABF is staffed with unit engineers (such as radar, navigation, and so on), and borrows programmers as needed from another group within the corporation.

For systems A, B, and F, a separate system definition contract preceded the development competition. Except for documentation requirements, however, few software issues are usually discussed in the development proposals. By contrast, the system definition contract for system B led to a software specification that contained functional specifications, processing algorithms, and input- and output-data requirements. In other words, certain details of the software design were available well before the development contract was awarded.

Before submitting proposals, ABF contacts several potential subcontractors to discuss draft specifications, including those for software. This is done to encourage early proposals from each potential subcontractor. These discussions are vital to cost estimating, especially for determining the size of various subsystems. The technical feasibility of the specification is also examined, and the expertise of each potential subcontractor is assessed in the relevant technologies.

Controls on changes in requirements are initiated internally. In earlier programs, each change took from three to six months to make. Eventually, such complexity generated an appeal by the contractor for a reduction in reporting requirements. The Air Force agrees to compromise mainly because of scarce SPO manpower resources. The result (for systems B and F) was to require only the top-level flowcharts. Delivery of the rest of the software documentation was delayed until the start of integration testing. Thus, much of the detailed information generated during the production of the proposal—especially regarding software—was not supplied to the Air Force during the early development period.

Contractor ABF supports several specialty groups in such areas as radar, navigation, controls and displays, and weapon systems. An integration team is formed to coordinate the inputs and the outputs of all groups to generate one coherent picture. Such groups deal with technical issues and lead the way toward developing the integration block diagrams (IBD) mentioned earlier. These are diagrams similar to flowcharts that show how a user might view the operation of each mission capability. IBD's evolve iteratively over time. Initially rough and short on detail, they are eventually used as input to specifications as they become more and more specific and accurate.

These groups are formed before a proposal is generated and are composed of senior technical managers. Most groups include people with software expertise, but such people usually do not have formal training in computer science. Rather, they are unit specialists who understand software as it applies to their individual areas. A radar unit engineer, for example, might understand the software needed for the specialized processing requirements of radar. The first group products are procurement lists that are later associated with the evolving IBDs to supply needed detail on how to accomplish the required functions. IBDs indicate only where computers are involved in a particular mission segment; they do not indicate how the computer is involved and, in particular, do not deal with the specifics of individual programs or algorithms.

Contractor ABF has apparently assisted the Air Force in developing new RFPs on an informal basis for some time. The Air Force provides draft RFPs to solicit prototype specifications; these, in turn, help them evaluate potential acquisition programs. Typically, this involves white papers and unsolicited proposals produced by contractors. Thus, the contractors are usually involved with an emerging program well before the Air Force decides to release an RFP.

Once there is firm information that the government will, in fact, pursue an acquisition, the contractor's teams grow larger very quickly. The original management cast provides leadership for several new groups in specific technical areas; these groups in turn split into subgroups, acquiring people in various specialties as necessary. The technical groups often continue to grow throughout the full-scale development period.

ABF also obtains initial cost estimates from potential subcontractors and from their own contracts office. Their biggest concerns at this time are the gross costs associated with size, weight, and power requirements. ABF prepares draft purchase specifications for use by potential subcontractors. (As indicated earlier, however, the more aggressive subcontractors have already influenced the emerging specifications.) Responses to draft specifications are generated by evaluating preliminary cost and design information. The specifications are periodically revised, and more trade-off analyses are done. As these estimates evolve, the development project begins to take on firm boundaries.

If ABF makes a decision to pursue the contract, they continue to develop the prototype proposal and try to anticipate what the RFP will look like. They work hard to get a head start on building the proposal, but for all this effort, there may be very few pages in the proposal dealing explicitly with software.

Once an RFP is received, ABF will form several specialty groups, as needed, to deal with each major section. Their draft proposal is essentially divided into a number of ''books,'' each comprising a separate area specification. ''Book captains'' are responsible for getting these documents in on schedule so they can be reviewed by technical management. The project groups are motivated to get early reviews and to do good initial work because schedules are affected by any adverse review. This tension between group leaders and technical management is seen as an important contributor to the quality of a proposal.

ABF requires certain preliminary documentation from potential subcontractors before a proposal is submitted, but it may not actually receive this documentation until three to four months after the contract has been awarded. It may then be too late for the prime contractor to derive any benefit from the subcontractor's specifications, since the prime contractor moved forward on the proposal much more rapidly than the subcontractor did. Some respondents felt, however, that if subcontractors were to submit rough documentation earlier, it might be ony marginally useful because of a lack of detail.

ABF continues its design work during the contract negotiation period, changing and clarifying the original proposal and continuing to develop the software specifications. At the same time, they begin to generate the interface block diagrams. As mentioned earlier, when there is a separate system definition contract there are usually fairly detailed software specifications by the time the full-scale development contract is awarded; a detailed set of interface block diagrams may also be available. ABF personnel emphasized that contractors are always involved between one and three years before the formal RFP appears, because they need to understand how the system is to work before they can develop their proposal.

After the contract is awarded, both ABF and the customer conduct informal, but frequent, reviews of the evolving specifications for each area. Formal reviews act as the major milestones around which work is structured. Draft software product specifications are available soon after the award, and some coding may begin. Management supports progress by cross-checks that are frequently very detailed.

Figure B–1 summarizes the software development process as undertaken by contractor ABF.

Contractor E

Important influences on contractor E's software development process are visible as far back as the mid-1960s, when they were involved in another

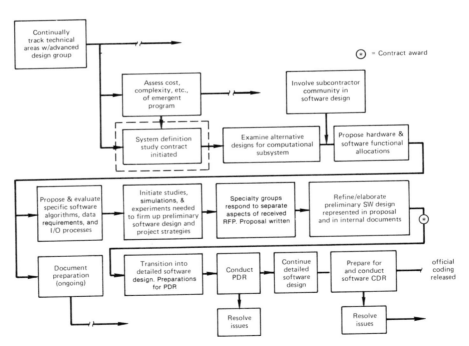

Figure B–1. Embedded Software Development: Contractor ABF

program. For various reasons, that program was considered a software disaster. The software interfaces, for example, were so complex that even routine maintenance was difficult, and problems were extremely difficult to troubleshoot because the system architecture obscured the sources of faults.

In the late 1960s, E and another contractor were awarded small contracts to demonstrate new technologies that had potential military applications. Government interest in this area continued throughout 1971. In April 1972, both contractors won continuation contracts from the Air Force to develop prototype systems. The Air Force also set up a small pre–program office organization to work with the competing contractor teams and to develop performance specifications against which to compare the prototype systems. A competitive evaluation was scheduled for early 1974.

In 1972, E formed an internally funded study group to consider the potential roles of the new system in greater detail. This group played a major role in generating software requirements for what eventually became a major acquisition program. (This is discussed in more detail shortly.)

In 1974, E received an additional $4 million for preparing full-scale development proposals; in July of that year they organized a formal group for that purpose. A prime consideration during the proposal phase was the development of a system specification. A large number of people were drawn from the internal study effort to produce this document. Participating, at one time or another, were experts in software development, operations, support, and so on—experts who had already been working on the potential system for at least two years. During that time, the group had produced informal documentation in the form of working notes, talking papers, and charts that had evolved into a system definition. This was now worked into the draft specification.

The proposal contained a preliminary software design, an initial allocation of software functions, early decisions about the number and size of computer hardware items, preliminary interface methodologies and data, initial flowcharts, and so on. This information was embodied in a large collection of documents, including the following:

A system specification containing a preliminary breakdown of the major software requirements.

A computer program development plan.

A preliminary software development specification for each computer subsystem.

A preliminary interface specification.

A relatively complete management proposal.

Software cost data.

Internal documents comprising precursors to a software product specification.

In addition, the group had formalized lessons learned on earlier projects into a document that examined past problems and proposed means for avoiding them. This well-thumbed document was an important influence on the system software architecture and on its functional breakdown. Computer hardware specifications, also available, had been under development for some time because hardware cost information was required for the proposal.

E had also identified the system components to be subcontracted and potential vendors for each. Preliminary specifications were written incorporating requirements that, while allowing a subcontractor to employ its comparative technological advantage, nevertheless guaranteed E's overall control of the software development program. These specifications identified inputs to be supplied to, and outputs expected from, the subsystems. This approach resulted from an early decision to define the major subsystems as autonomous entities. Thus, subsystem X would incorporate processing capabilities sufficient to supply immediately usable data to the mission computer, rather than "raw" data requiring preprocessing. In this way, E could test the delivered product with easily generated inputs that were to produce specific, easily checked outputs. The responsibilities for problems were also clear, and E could avoid sometimes lengthy and costly finger-pointing episodes.

Later versions of the preliminary software specifications contained few substantive changes from the initial documents; the main impression is one of gradually increasing detail. In some cases, however, detail actually diminished in later documents. For example, software flowcharts included in the original specifications were not included in subsequent versions. E had submitted flowcharts with its proposal in order to convey that they had given considerable thought to software design. However, after the contract was awarded they questioned the logic of providing such detail so early. E argued for delaying flowchart-level documentation until the the actual software design was available. The Air Force, having been bitten in the past by insufficient software documentation, was nervous at first. E won the point by agreeing in writing to supply such documentation as part of the software product specifications—amounting to a partial waiver of certain documentation requirements.

The 1974 competition pitted the two prototypes against the customer's performance criteria (not against one another). E emerged as the winner with respect to prototype performance and several other indicators of contractor capability. However, this competition gave little information about E's capabilities in the software area, because the prototypes embodied only enough software to enable performance data to be collected.

The development contract was awarded to E in January of 1975, and work began immediately on adding more detail to the existing software specifications. The two major sources of guidance available besides the earlier internal-study effort were the lessons learned form earlier programs and E's continuing involvement with a relevant research program at one of the Air Force's laboratories. The latter work provided information on advanced concepts and capabilities and had already resulted in certain aids to software testing and integration.

Other inputs to the software-development process were (1) a core set of roles and capabilities for the system as a whole, (2) strong and informed management, and (3) a clear picture of the specific roles to be played by the product. The latter two inputs provided philosophical guidance needed to integrate the various technical aspects and helped resolve technical and managerial problems that cropped up during the development period.

E also called attention to several advantages of their internal studies. First, they provided a head start on preparing a timely response to the RFP. Second, understanding the breadth as well as the depth of the anticipated product permitted a coordinated development strategy. Third, the studies generated information useful for reducing some of the technical and managerial uncertainties of both E and the customer.

The first internal study group was organized in 1972. It included (1) experts in computer hardware and software, (2) management representatives from the contractor, the user, and the pre-program office, and (3) a number of representatives from vendors. Thus, from the earliest conceptions of system E, the necessary manpower, skills, technical information, and experience were available. Initial discussions dealt with system/subsystem processing. One of the lessons learned was that the subsystem interfaces should be as simple as possible. Thus, the group created an architecture of minimally connected autonomous subsystems with moderate program size and clean straightforward code. (This lends support to the hypothesis that, for software, early requirements analysis and software design tasks are, as a practical matter, carried out simultaneously.)

The original group gradually disaggregated into smaller specialized teams, each formed to develop and evaluate concepts in specific areas. Other groups identified appropriate algorithms, tested them in various ways (including by computer simulation), and suggested the adoption of some and the modification of others. Where necessary, development was initiated for new algorithms. This indicates that at least some of the necessary support software was available (or was developed with discretionary funds) prior to a formal Defense Department go-ahead on system development. All of the major software products were concurrently discussed, coordinated, and engineered in an attempt to guarantee trouble-free development and integration and economical life-cycle support. E feels that such a "stew-pot" environment buys important information-transfer benefits for the various software categories under consideration.

The various groups met roughly once a week to present their progress to a red team of high-level technical and management personnel that continually reviewed the work of the individual design teams. Inputs were also received from the customer, contractors interested in potential subcontracts, and vendors of pertinent equipment. Comparisons were made pitting the functional capabilities of similar existing systems against what was, by this time, a fairly clear picture of the roles to be played by the new system. In this way, software requirements in a number of areas (performance, function, interface, and so on) were proposed, verified, coordinated with decisions in other areas, and informally documented—all by mid-1973, one and one-half years before the development contract was awarded.

By late 1973, a core set of software requirements had been produced and described to E's management and to the Air Force. Moreover, the overall software architecture, its functional allocations, and certain backup-mode and error-processing decisions had been agreed to. The outlines of a potential RFP had also emerged during this period, so work gradually came to reflect shared perceptions about operational roles, specific capabilities, and overall computational responsibilities.

The relatively sudden decision by the Air Force to pursue system development led to a very difficult period requiring a quick transition from technology demonstration to full-scale development. The knowledge developed during E's internal studies contributed to easing this transition.

After the contract was awarded, E began to add detail to the preliminary software specifications submitted with the proposal. For example, where the preliminary specification treated inputs for a particular module in one or two general paragraphs, expanded versions discussed both internal and external inputs in greater and greater detail, eventually (in most cases) down to the bit level. This expansion drew on the personal experience of senior engineers organized in specialized teams formed explicitly to design software for the mission computer.

Software specifications evolved gradually as software designs were refined. As new information accumulated, periodic revisions were made to specification documents. Software designs for each subsystem were pursued concurrently, documented as decisions were made, coordinated with one another and with the evolving interface specifications, and subjected to regular and frequent scrutiny by peer groups from related projects and by top engineering management. Software requirements were expected to reach final form only in the software-product specifications, which were produced while the actual code is being written.

Initial efforts tended to focus on the preliminary design review. The inputs to this review were the software development specifications (expanded in detail, but without flowcharts) and an early draft of the software-product specifications, produced from informal documentation. E personnel prepared for the PDR by rehearsing before red teams made up of members from other teams and from senior management. Such rehearsals also provided participants with information about other parts of the project, thus aiding coordination.

Just prior to the review, E had begun to refine the design of the mission computer's software components. The process involved decomposing general functions into increasingly more specific components. In this way, the detailed software design emerged as a group of computer program components. Each group was associated with one or more computer program configuration items. As the preliminary review approached, a final internal review and a design walk-through were held.

The next focus of attention was the critical design review. In this review, the functional requirements are gone over in detail by E project management and then by the Air Force. For software, it is aimed at evaluating how well the contractor has mapped system functions into computer program components.

Between the two reviews, the software development specifications were brought to a stage where they were useful to those responsible for software test design. E made a point of the level of detail in the specification. A document without too much detail provides a more stable basis for the design and early implementation stages of software development. One reason is that the frequent low-level changes that crop up during that period are less likely to to conflict with, and require changes to, specifications at the right level of detail. This is important in view of E's approach to documentation, but may be less a factor in other approaches to software development. By the time of the critical review, the software specifications had progressed to the point where programmers could use them for producing code. They contained flowcharts identifying individual modules to be programmed, references to necessary algorithms, and the input and output data required for each module.

As coding proceeded, the engineers (though still acting as consultants to the programmers) focused most of their attention on test planning. At first, these efforts were aimed at informal debugging carried out as program modules became available. Software changes resulting from this experience were documented in the concurrently evolving software-product specifications.

The program office and E agreed that software changes were to be minimized during the full-scale development period. This agreement was translated into formal configuration controls. Potential changes in software design brought to light during coding had to traverse a formal—and documented—approval path before being incorporated into the specifications. This acted as a disincentive to change, and E hoped that, as a result, only important changes would take place during the development period.

Eight major versions of the code had been produced before software testing got underway. Program listings were submitted to an experienced red team who identified the requirements actually met by the code. These were divided into formal requirements, implicit (that is, derived) requirements, and "nice features." Any left over were summarily deleted. The Air Force was given the option of accepting the niceties or not, with the understanding that they would have some impact on overall system performance. At the same time, programmers worked to reduce the size and improve the performance of the remaining code. In combination, these efforts constituted a production engineering stage for the mission software and reduced the size of the final package by some 9000 words without sacrificing functionality.

Figure B–2 summarizes the software development process as undertaken by Contractor E.

Contractor H

Contractor H uses a requirements task force to look at desired system-level performance, and moves gradually from there to defining various subsystems. The task force operates under a system engineering manager and includes experts in hardware, software, and systems analysis. One tool used by this group is called a systems sequence diagram. Diagrams are first drawn at a very high level, but as concepts are elaborated, they become increasingly more detailed and more representative of the final implemetation. Typically, the first group of diagrams requires about two months to develop. By the time a revised set is complete, detailed charts for all pertinent areas are available. At this point, the systems analysts decide which specific functions will be assigned to hardware and which

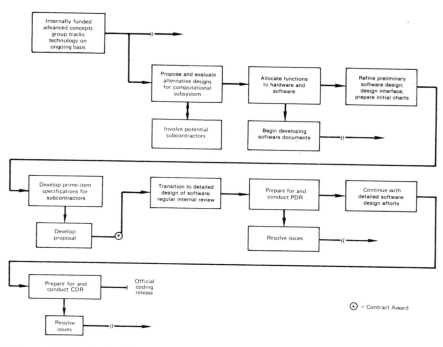

Figure B–2. Embedded Software Development: Contractor E

to software. These lists are circulated and carefully reviewed. There was thus an early application of software expertise, in marked contrast to other programs.

One of the most difficult tasks is to control changes to the software. The systems sequence charts, very useful in this regard, are used to implement configuration management requirements imposed by the Air Force's change-documentation regulations. Each functional group producing a chart contains experts in the mission area, in software, and in hardware. These people are located physically near to one another and work closely together to understand the software and hardware functional paths that pertain to their misssion area.

However, the procedure just described was not followed rigorously on the system H program. Because of schedule pressures, software development for system H ran much more in parallel than for earlier systems. System H software personnel used what is known as milestone documentation. Such documentation is roughly equivalent in content to customary development specifications, but does not completely satisfy more customary documentation standards. The contractor also developed a separate but somewhat overlapping set of internal documents. Some Air Force support groups are now asking for this internal documentation as well as, or instead of, the documentation to be delivered with the software. One Air Force respondent suggested that the latter is used for training and for developing maintenance procedures, but that it is most useful because of the discipline it imposes on the contractor during software development.

The time between submitting the proposal and being awarded the contract was spent revising the first milestone document, which was aimed primarily at the preliminary design review. At the same time (and in parallel with finalizing the draft documents), the contractor prepared a software integration requirements document. This was written by system engineering personnel using as inputs the first milestone document and other system-level architecture information. It dealt primarily with the allocation of functions to hardware and software, imposing detailed requirements in both areas.

In theory, the first milestone document and the integration document are used to create a second milestone document—a software concept paper containing flowcharts and narratives describing each function or operational mode that the software will support. In practice the integration and second milestone documents were produced in parallel rather than sequentially because the project is generally on a tight schedule.

Taken together, the first two milestone documents were approximately equivalent to a software-development specification. They contained block diagrams and specifications regarding performance and functions. Each function included a list of inputs and was described with logic diagrams. A lot of experience is brought to bear in producing these documents, and a certain amount was learned in the process. The two milestone documents were then used as inputs for preparing the development proposal, which was submitted in March 1978.

The management of program H is based on informal technical interchanges between personnel of the program office and the contractor. Many of these meetings focus on software. The participants oversee certain crucial activities and solve problems that crop up along the way. Program office personnel are augmented at these meetings by technical support contractor personnel; in general, though, meetings all tend to involve the same people. Thus, as time goes on, a relatively close-knit friendly, nonadversary team is formed.

Contractor H also maintains contact with Air Force Logistics Command and with the primary users of the system. In fact, the users were heavily involved in the system definition phase and generated the first set of system requirements. Logistics Command usually has a relatively limited early role, but is expected to become more involved as the production and support phases approach.

The contractor draws an organizational distinction between systems engineering and software engineering. This, and the existence of the two levels of documentation mentioned earlier, is said to improve management oversight of software activities.

One more document is produced in preparation for the preliminary review—the third milestone document. It is the software-to-software and software-to-people interface specification; it also contains descriptions of several important system data bases.

The preliminary review consisted of many briefings and other meetings, staggered so that various program office personnel could attend those relevant to their interests. For each functional area, the contractor discussed the requirements of the system, their interpretation of the requirements, and the approach to be taken in their satisfaction. H's representation at these meetings included systems, software support, and hardware specialists. The review was seen as a working session, not as a political event as with some other programs. The Air Force had 300 or 400 specific questions for H's consideration and resolution. Most came from an earlier document review and identified problems in a number or areas. Approximately forty issues relating to software were raised, or roughly 10 percent of the total.

After the review, the contractor began producing several additional milestone documents. Some of the same people were involved at this stage; along with them came a number of less senior personnel. Each major function of the computational sybsystem was to be implemented by a number of separate computer program components that together performed the needed tasks. A milestone specification was written for each individual component; each such document was equivalent to a software-product specification. With these documents, the programming task became relatively straightforward.

The new documents were prerequisites to the critical design review. Programming is usually authorized after the design specifications have been formally accepted; however, because of schedule pressures, programming for some system H modules got underway well before the review. The contractor was taking a risk by starting early—if the system did not pass the review, necessary changes could require a backup in the design path and, possibly, reprogramming. However, with good interaction between the program office and the contractor, reviews can be routine, and the risks of early programming can be minimized.

Figure B–3 summarizes the software development process as undertaken by contractor H.

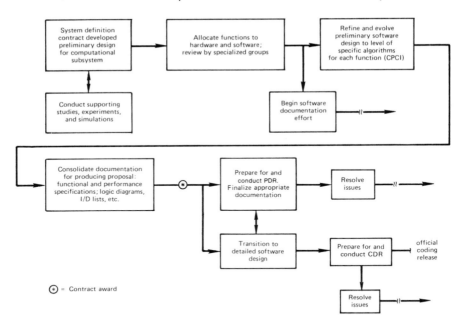

Figure B–3. Embedded Software Development: Contractor H

Contractor DG

For this contractor, defining software requirements starts with the major elements of the job to be done—for example, the equipment, the power requirements, and the major computer algorithms. During proposal generation, specialist groups are formed to discuss the system elements that will have software requirements. Senior technicians from each key area engage in informal talks that result in high-level functional architectures. Hardware and software allocations emerge during this time. System D, for example, had a long history of such discussions; proposal-level specifications were developed over a period of approximately three years. Part of this effort was funded by a precontract award, but it was not considered to be a formal system definition contract.

Because the Air Force expects a certain level of design detail in proposals, several potential software subcontractors participate in these meeings. Proposals from DG discuss system requirements as related to performance, as well as whether or not the envisioned computational subsystem will have enough storage capacity and processing speed to do the job. Software implementation details are left for later documents. Any decision to use a high-order language is recorded in the proposal; certain functional software architecture decisions are discussed there as well. By the time a proposal is submitted, details of the software implementation are usually under consideration. DG uses the time between the submission of their proposal and the awarding of the contract to shore up known weaknesses in their proposal and to prepare to defend positions taken in that document that could lead to conflict with the customer.

Immediately after the contract for system D was awarded, the software subcontractor (SS) and DG began to refine and extend the software architecture represented in the proposal. This was done by senior systems-level people, not by programmers. In fact, software expertise was not represented in the group at all except to the extent that some hardware personnel were familiar with it; no programming-level decisions were made.

The software effort was not formally managed at first, and even though parts of the effort (such as documentation) grew more formal over time, decision-making mechanisms at the working level remained informal. All decisions were, however, reviewed by DG's management.

Six months into the development phase, the SS produced a draft of the software-development specification. The preliminary design review, however, had been carried out about three months earlier, and although the specifications evolved continuously throughout the full-scale development period, the software design was never baselined.

The software-product specifications were available within about five months; they should have been available at critical design review time. The time lag was due mainly to a compressed schedule.

Six months after the contract was awarded, a major engineering change was approved. Because of this change, the necessary storage increased to the maximum available on the single-processor configuration previously selected, thereby using up previously reserved spare capacity. The primary impact, however, was on software. In the middle of designing an already complex system, the contractors had to undersatnd, design, develop, and integrate a large number of new mission requirements. This caused not only considerable reworking of the original software requirements, but concurrent formulation of the software requirements for the new mission. It was well into the testing phase before DG and the Air Force came to any sort of an agreement on exactly what the new software functions were to be and how the user would employ them. There was no real appreciation of the inherent complexity of the new combined mission or of how difficult the change would be to integrate into system D's original design.

The impact was huge. Storage capacity was exceeded, the schedule was delayed, and the capabilities of the equipment used for integration and testing were strained. There were also disparate expectations as to the redefined system's capabilities. The user, for example, expected a fully automated system, whereas the contractor wrote the engineering change proposal thinking in terms of semiautomated concepts. A major component of the impact was dissent among all participants, pressure for new capabilities, and increased turmoil throughout the program, all of which gave the impression of inadequate planning, faulty implementation, and a general lack of appropriate guidance.

The Air Force and the contractor interacted frequently between the preliminary and critical design reviews; this included occasional informal presentations of program status. The critical design review was supported in part by a draft software product specification. At the time, it contained only architectural information and ignored individual program modules (the usual focus of such documents). Those details were included just after the critical design review, but it should be noted that the software-product specifications for the new mission software were behind schedule, and that this implies a double documentation effort.

The critical design review did not include a technical review of the software design. It was seen as a formal milestone: well attended, but of little substantive value to either the Air Force or the contractor. Furthermore, no discipline had been applied to the software requirements or design processes, either internally by the contractors or externally by the Air Force.

DG used a system engineering organization concerned with hardware-software interfaces, communications, calibration, tracking-and-classification missions, and man-machine interfaces. There was also a software manager who monitored the subcontractors' performance. The software subcontractor felt that software engineering support was a very important part of his company's original proposal. However, they allowed themselves to be talked out of the task; the prime contractor had argued that they (DG) would do that job. In fact, the software engineering task eventually fell to SS, but by then its software-engineering budget allocation had been deleted. Software engineering turned out to be the weakest area in the contract.

A major software problem came to light during the integration period. The software subcontractor had committed itself to a very advanced algorithm on the word of a highly-thought-of employee. Although there was concern from the beginning about its feasibility, the originator of the idea reported directly to corporate management, bypassing his company's software management cadre. He was very articulate and a good defender of his concepts; no one within SS would take the risk of formally questioning his expertise, his concept, or its ultimate utility to the D program. As a result, the system was well into integration testing before the situation was fully understood. At this point, the program had to be refocused to use a less risky technology. In retrospect, the virtually complete failure to manage an individual technician significantly affected software costs and the entire program's schedule. The solution, once it was available, was relatively straightforward; furthermore, the basic software design remained intact.

The software group at SS did the original top-level software design. This group discussed the interfaces, the data bases, and the functions to be supported by software. They used an iterative process, developing informally documented models of increasing specificity while retaining a focus at the overall functional level. They generated software module transition charts called "spaghetti charts"; these were presented at the critical design review. It is important to note that the SS did much of the software requirements and design work during the proposal stage; but, since technical accountability had not yet been established, the work was not presented to DG early enough to be used in the proposal submitted to the Air Force.

DG had daily contact with SS's programmers and engineers, but Air Force oversight of software development was limited to the formal reviews. The one software expert working in the program office was interested mainly in requirements specification; implementation plans were rarely discussed. As a consequence, the review procedure failed to discover that, as designed, the software would exceed the storage capacity of the chosen single processor. To make it work, the code had to be resegmented and overlayed very late in the program. The temporary addition of a second machine helped the testing situation somewhat, but real-time problems remained.

The president of SS took special interest in program D from the beginning and made some recommendations that, because they were ignored, had decidedly negative cost impacts. He recommended, for example, that since high-rate data collection was not important in the user community, it should not be included in system D's requirements. It was included nevertheless, and the software and hardware associated with it are now viewed as contribtutors to unnecessary cost growth.

With respect to machine size, SS was lucky, in a sense. Having originally overspecified, they had spare speed and processing power when the engineering change came in. As a result, there was little performance degradation on the major missions. As mentioned earlier, it was necessary to overlay the software; however, this posed few technical problems. Contractor DG could have been hurt much worse by the ramifications of

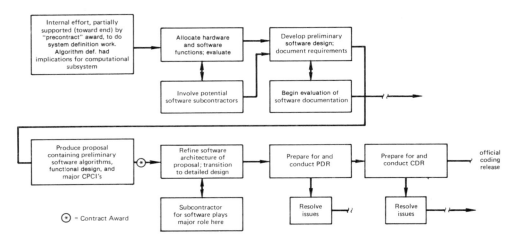

Figure B–4. Embedded Software Development: Contractor DG

the late-arriving change. They were saved by the software subcontractor's professionalism and competence.

Figure B–4 summarizes the software development process as undertaken by contractor DG.

Bibliography

Air Force Avionics Laboratory. August 1977. Software cost estimating methodology. Technical report AFAL–TR–77–66.

Ansoff, H.I., and Brandenburg, R.G. 1971. A language for organization design. *Management Science,* no. 17, parts 1 and 2.

Aviation Week and Space Technology. 16 February 1981. Broad technology gains made.

Baker, F.T. 1972. Chief programmer team management of production programming. *IBM Systems Journal,* vol. 11, no. 1.

Barbee, G.M. October 1978. A study of embedded computer system software acquisition management and recommendations to improve development visibility. Air Force Institute of Technology, report no. AFIT/GSM/SM/78S–1.

Bell, T.E., et al. January 1977. An extendable approach to computer-aided software requirements engineering. *IEEE Transactions on Software Engineering,* vol. SE–3, no. 1.

Blau, P.M., and Scott, W.R. 1962. *Formal organizations.* San Francisco: Chandler Publishing Co.

Burr, W.E., et al. September 1977. Summary of the final report of the Army/Navy computer family architecture selection committee. Research and development technical report, ECOM 4525.

Byrne, W.E., et al. December 1978. Draft Data Item Description (DID) for Software Acquisition Resource Expenditure (SARE) reporting. MITRE Corporation, working paper WP–21975, vol. 1.

Chandler, A.D. 1962. *Strategy and structure: Chapters in the history of the industrial enterprise.* New York: Anchor.

Child, J., and Mansfield, R. 1972. Technology, size and organization structure. *Sociology,* no. 6.

Child, J. 1973. Predicting and understanding organization structure. *Administrative Science Quarterly,* no. 18.

Davis, M.R., Glaseman, S., and Stanley, W.L. 1982. Acquisition and support of embedded computer system software. Santa Monica, CA, Rand Corporation, R–2831–AF.

DeMarco, T. 1979. *Structured analysis and system specification.* Englewood Cliffs, NJ: Prentice-Hall, Inc.

DeRoze, B.C. October 1975. An introspective analysis of DoD weapon system software analysis. *Defense Management Journal.*

Dill, W.R. March 1958. Environment as an influence on managerial autonomy. *Administrative Science Quarterly,* vol. 2.

Douglas, F.E. 1980. Embedded software acquisition management. In *Proceedings, NAECON,* Dayton Convention Center, vol. 3.

Drezner, S.M., et al. April 1976. The computer resources management study. Santa Monica, CA, Rand Corporation, R–1855/1–PR.

Driscoll, A.J. November 1976. Software visibility for the program manager. Defense Systems Management College, study project report 76–2.

Emery, F.E., and Trist, E.L. February 1965. Causal texture of organizational environments. *Human Relations.*

Etzioni, A. 1975. *A Comparative Analysis of Complex Organizations* (revised). New York: The Free Press.

Fisher, D.A. June 1976. A common programming language for the Department of Defense—Background and technical requirements. Institute for Defense Analysis, P–1191, AD–A028297.

Glaseman, S., and Davis, M.R. March 1980. Software requirements for embedded computers: A preliminary report. Santa Monica, CA, Rand Corporation, R–2567–AF.

Glass, R.L. May 1980. Real time: The ''lost world'' of software debugging and testing. *Communications of the Association for Computing Machinery,* vol. 23, no. 5.

Glore, J.B. 1978. ESD software cost prediction aids project: Interim results and plans. MITRE Corporation, working paper WP–22029, no. 17.

Good, D., London, R., and Bledsoe, W.W. March 1975. An interactive program verification system. *IEEE Transactions on Software Engineering,* vol. SE–1, no. 1.

Hawley, A.H. 1950. *Human Ecology.* New York: Ronald Press.

Head, R.V. February 1981. Federal information systems management. Brookings Institution.

Hickson, D.J. et al. 1969. Operations technology and organization structure: An empirical reappraisal. *Administrative Science Quarterly,* no. 14.

Hosier, W.A. June 1961. Pitfalls and safeguards in real-time digital systems with emphasis on programming. *IRE Transactions on Engineering Management.*

House, R. June 1980. Comments on program specification and testing. *Communications of the Association for Competing Machinery,* vol. 23, no. 6.

Howden, W. 1978. Theoretical and empirical studies of program testing. In *Proceedings of the 3rd International Conference on Software Engineering.*

Hughes, E.C. 1952. The sociological study of work. *American Journal of Sociology,* no. 57.

Jackson, J.H., and Morgan, C.P. 1978. *Organization Theory.* New Jersey: Prentice-Hall.

Johns Hopkins University Applied Physics Laboratory. May 1975. DOD weapons system software management study.

Katz, D., and Kahn, R. 1966. *The Social Psychology of Organizations.* New York: John Wiley.

Lehman, J.H. January 1979. How software projects are really managed. *Datamation Magazine.*

Levine, S., and White, P.E. March 1961. Exchange as a conceptual framework for the study of interorganizational relationships. *Administrative Science Quarterly,* vol. 5.

Logicon Corporation. June 1976. Management guide to avionics software acquisition: An overview of software development and management. Technical report ASD-TR-76-11, vol. 1.

Losi, D. November 1977. The program manager and the matrix organization. Defense Systems Management College, study project report 77-2.

Marks, K.E. November 1980. Estimating avionics software development cost. Santa Monica, CA, Rand Corporation, N-1603-AF.

McGowen, C.L., and Kelley, J.R. 1975. *Top down structured programming techniques.* New York: Petrocelli/Charter.

Miller, E.J., and Rice, A.K. 1963. *Systems in Organizations: The Control of Task and Sentient Boundaries.* London: Tarustock.

MITRE Corporation. May 1975. DOD weapons system software acquisition and management study.

National Academy of Sciences. 1977. Operational software management and development for U.S. Air Force computer systems. Washington, D.C.

Naur, P., and Randell, B. 1968. Software engineering. NATO Scientific Affairs Division, Brussels.

Parsons, T. 1960. *Structure and process in modern society.* New York: The Free Press.

Peters, L. November 1978. Relating software requirements and design. In *Performance Evaluation and Review/Software Engineering Notes.* Joint publication, *Proceedings of the Software Quality and Assurance Workshop.*

Pfeffer, J., and Salancik, G.R. 1978. *The external control of organizations.* New York: Harper and Row.

Pugh, D.S., et al. 1969. The context of organization structures. *Administrative Science Quarterly,* no. 14.

Putnam, W.D. August 1972. The evolution of Air Force system acquisition management. Santa Monica, CA, Rand Corporation, R-868-PR.

Sethi, N.K. 1970. A research model to study the environmental factors in management. *Management International Review,* no. 10.

Starbuck, W.H. 1965. Organizational growth and development. In March, J.G., ed., *Handbook of organizations*. Chicago: Rand McNally.

Teichroew, D., et al. 1975. An introduction to PSL/PSA. University of Michigan at Ann Arbor, ISDDS working paper no. 86.

Thompson, J.D. 1967. *Organizations in action*. New York: McGraw-Hill Book Co.

Trist, E.L., and Bamforth, K.W. February 1951. Some social and psychological consequences of the long-wall method of coal getting. *Human Relations*, no. 4.

U.S. Department of Defense. October 1968. Specification practices. Military Standard 490.

U.S. Air Force. December 1970. Configuration management practices for systems, equipment, munitions and computer programs. Military Standard 483.

U.S. Air Force. August 1971. Policies, responsibilities, and procedures for obtaining new and improved operational capabilities. Air Force Regulation 57–1.

U.S. Air Force. July 1974. Configuration management. Air Force Regulation 65–3.

U.S. Air Force. September 1975. Management of computer resources in systems. Air Force Regulation 800–14, vols. 1 and 2.

U.S. Air Force. June 1976. Technical reviews and audits for systems, equipment, and computer programs. Military Standard 1521A.

U.S. Government Accounting Office. 21 September 1978. NORAD'S information processing improvement program: Will it enhance mission capability? LCD–78–117.

Ware, W.H. April 1978. Unpublished issue paper on acquisition and support of computer based defense systems.

Wasserman, A.I. and Freeman, P. August 1978. Software engineering education: Status and prospects. In *Proceedings of the IEEE*, vol. 66, no. 8.

Weick, K.E. 1969. *The social psychology of organizing*. Reading, MA: Addison-Wesley.

Woodward, J. 1958. *Management and technology: Problems of progress in industry* (series no. 3). London: HMSO.

Woodward, J. 1965. Industrial organization: Theory and practice. London: Oxford University Press.

Woodward, J. 1970. Industrial organization: Behavior and control. London: Oxford University Press.

Yourdon, E., and Constantine, L. 1975. *Structured design*. Englewood Cliffs, NJ: Prentice-Hall, Inc.

Index

About the Author

Steven Glaseman is currently a research scientist with Teledyne Systems Company in Northridge, California. Before joining Teledyne, he was on the staff of the Rand Corporation in Santa Monica, California. Dr. Glaseman has written primarily on the topics of defense software acquisition, command and control systems analysis, and computer system security. Dr. Glaseman received the B.A. and M.S. degrees in psychology and systems engineering, respectively, and received the Ph.D. in policy analysis from the Rand Graduate Institute.